BLACKSMITH, BAKER, ROOFING-SHEET MAKER. . . .

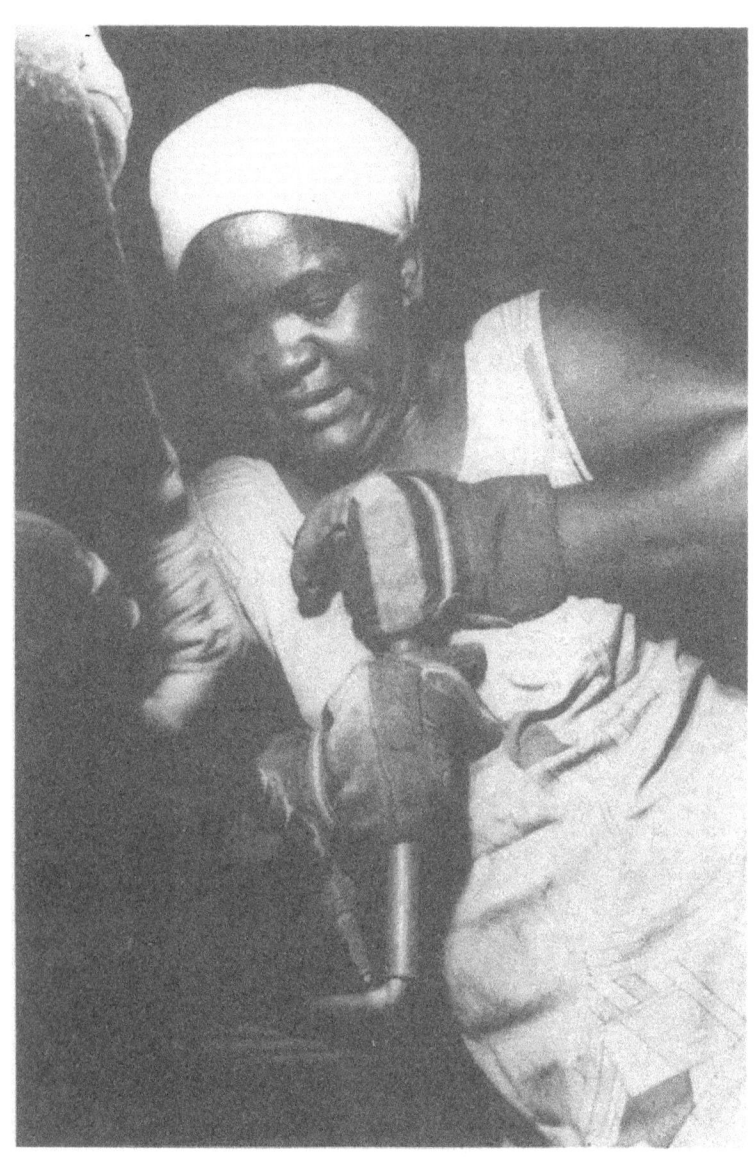

In some parts of the world women are blacksmiths.

Blacksmith, Baker, Roofing-sheet maker....

Employment for rural women in developing countries

MARILYN CARR

INTERMEDIATE TECHNOLOGY PUBLICATIONS

Practical Action Publishing Ltd
25 Albert Street, Rugby, CV21 2SD, Warwickshire, UK
www.practicalactionpublishing.com

© Intermediate Technology Publications 1984

First published 1984\Digitised 2013

ISBN 10: 0 9466 881 5 X
ISBN 13 Paperback: 9780946688159
ISBN Library Ebook: 9781780441757
Book DOI: https://doi.org/10.3362/9781780441757

All rights reserved. No part of this publication may be reprinted or reproduced or utilized in any form or by any electronic, mechanical, or other means, now known or hereafter invented, including photocopying and recording, or in any information storage or retrieval system, without the written permission of the publishers.

A catalogue record for this book is available from the British Library.

The authors, contributors and/or editors have asserted their rights under the Copyright Designs and Patents Act 1988 to be identified as authors of their respective contributions.

Since 1974, Practical Action Publishing has published and disseminated books and information in support of international development work throughout the world. Practical Action Publishing is a trading name of Practical Action Publishing Ltd (Company Reg. No. 01159018), the wholly owned publishing company of Practical Action. Practical Action Publishing trades only in support of its parent charity objectives and any profits are covenanted back to Practical Action (Charity Reg. No. 247257, Group VAT Registration No. 880 9924 76).

Reasonable efforts have been made to publish reliable data and information, but the author and publisher cannot assume responsibility for the validity of all materials or for the consequences of their use.

The manufacturer's authorised representative in the EU for product safety is Lightning Source France, 1 Av. Johannes Gutenberg, 78310 Maurepas, France. compliance@lightningsource.fr

Contents

Acknowledgements	ix
Illustrations	xi
Foreword by Dorienne Wilson-Smillie	xiii

CHAPTER I: NEW JOBS FOR OLD	1
1. *Why Do Rural Women Need Cash?*	2
2. *What is Wrong with Handicrafts?*	3
3. *What are the Alternatives?*	9
CHAPTER II: OPTIONS FOR EARNING	15
1. *Food, Drink and Tobacco*	15
Fish Smoking in Ghana	16
Gari Processing in Ghana	18
Oil Processing in Sierra Leone	19
Oil Processing in Upper Volta	22
Coconut Sweets in Guyana	23
Corn and Cheese Biscuits in Honduras	25
Spices and Pickles in Bangladesh	26
Pappad Rolling in India	28
Puffed Rice in Bangladesh	30
A Bakery in Kenya	31
A Bakery in Botswana	32
Solar-dried Coconut in Bangladesh	34
Mango Purée in Honduras	37
Fruit and Vegetable Preserving in Honduras	38
Ready-to-Eat Infant Food Mix in India	39
Palmwine in Nigeria	40
Banana Chips in Papua New Guinea	41
Summary	43

2. *Cloth, Clothing and Fibres*	43
Wool Spinning in India	45
Spinning Muslin Yarn in India	49
Tie and Dye Co-operative in Tanzania	50
Dyeing in Mali and the Gambia	51
Carpet Weaving in Iran	52
Spinning in Upper Volta	54
Broadloom Weaving in Ghana	55
Spinning Silk in Bangladesh	56
Tailoring and Sewing Co-operatives in Tanzania	58
Textiles in Swaziland	59
School Uniforms in Botswana	60
Fishing-net Manufacture in India	61
Rope Making in Sri Lanka	63
Summary	65
3. *Building Materials, Housing and Household Goods*	66
Sisal-Cement Roofing Sheets in Kenya	68
Stove Factories in Indonesia	70
Stove Builders in the Sahel	72
Soap-making Co-operative in Tanzania	73
Soap Making in Mali	74
Caustic Potash Making in Ghana	79
Summary	80
4. *Other Consumer Goods*	81
Day-care Centre Equipment in Jamaica	83
Hospital Equipment in Bangladesh	86
Traditional Medicines in South India	87
Summary	88
5. *Other Productive Activities*	90
Winter Vegetables in Bangladesh	91
Vegetable Co-operatives in Botswana	94
Bananas in Samoa	96
Tree Planting in Kenya	97
Poultry Keeping in Kenya	99
Poultry Raising in Bangladesh	100
Goats and Kids in South India	100
Goat Rearing in Bangladesh	101

Beekeeping in Kenya	103
Fish Farming in Kenya	106
Summary	106
6. *Services*	107
Barefoot Vets in Bangladesh	108
Barefoot Mechanics in Nepal and Bangladesh	109
Barefoot Agriculturalists in The Gambia	110
Millers in Bangladesh	111
Custom Work in Bangladesh	112
Bus Service in Kenya	113
Summary	115
CHAPTER III: PROGRESS THROUGH LEARNING	117
1. General Overview	117
2. Factors in Success . . . and Problems	121
References for Case Studies	139
Sources for Further Information	143

ACKNOWLEDGEMENTS

The Intermediate Technology Development Group gratefully acknowledges the financial support of the Commonwealth Foundation in the preparation and publication of this book. The author wishes to acknowledge the contribution of Traude Rogers, who worked as research assistant in compiling the case study materials upon which the book is based.

Particular thanks are due to the following for the use of illustrations: John Swaby (cover, frontispiece and p. 85); Carla Risseeuw (p. 64); Gandhigram (p. 50); Lori Ann Thrupp (p. 98); UNICEF (p. 102); the Commonwealth Secretariat (p. 109); the World Bank (p. 104); Elizabeth O'Kelly (p. 113); and the Economic Commission of Africa (p. 119).

A NOTE ON CURRENCIES

Although the case studies described in this book cover a number of different years in the early 1970s and early 1980s, the following conversion rates, dating from October 1983, will give the reader a general idea of the values involved. A note records recent major revaluations.

	£ sterling	US $	
Bangladesh	37.25 taka	25.16	
Botswana	1.62 pula	0.87	
Ghana	45.15 cedis	30.50	(after the 90% 1983 revaluation)
India	15.27 rupees	10.32	
Indonesia	1,433.45 rupiyahs	979.80	
Kenya	20.25 shillings	13.68	
Nigeria	1.14 naira	0.76	
Swaziland	1.68 lilangeni	1.13	

Illustrations

	Page
In some parts of the world women are blacksmiths	Frontis.
The tourist and export market is already overcrowded	4
In India, women work alongside men	7
In Africa it is men who are the weavers	8
Women can make a wide range of commodities	11
Improved ovens in Ghana	17
Oil-presses in Sierra Leone.	21
Bangladeshi women preparing food for preservation	27
Production of dried coconut powder in Bangladesh	35
Sliced bananas laid out on trays to dry	42
Women in northern India, spinning wool	48
Muslin spinning in South India	50
Women in Bangladeshi silk production	57
Making fishing nets	62
A stage in coir processing, Sri Lanka	64
Sisal-cement roofing-sheets in Kenya	69
The village-level manufacture of ceramic stoves	72
The Markala soap co-operative in Mali	77
Women welders in Jamaica	85
Traditional medicines in South India	89
A women's vegetable co-operative	95
A Tree nursery in Kenya	98
Goat Rearing in India	102
Livestock as a source of income	104
Women caring for the village animals	109
Women can buy machinery	113
Women use tools, but are not taught to make them	119
Women in Guyana being taught to make solar driers	120

Foreword

All too often productive work for women, outside the home and the farm (the one non-income earning, and the other usually heavy-duty) is confined to handicrafts. The production of handicrafts can be a risky and unsatisfying business—at the mercy as it is of distant markets and sudden and unpredictable changes of fashion. So, while the Commonwealth Secretariat's Women and Development Programme is encouraging research into ways in which women's involvement in handicrafts production can be made more professional and profitable, and less risky, it has at the same time commissioned research into non-handicraft activities. And the survey published here shows both what a range of jobs women do - as well as in which areas of activity they are still, so far as we know, not involved.

The urgent quest for alternatives to handicraft production is neither new nor original, but the search, of which this book is a part, has gained impetus from expressions of discouragement and despair from countless Commonwealth women. Their desperation is such that, despite the failures, few women can afford to give up craft production. For many, the reality of a few pennies a year is better than nothing at all. And besides, everyone has heard about the successful project—always many miles away—where women earn money, feed their families, roof their houses and send their children to school. Who knows? Perhaps tomorrow it will be our turn . . .

Dreams can be dangerous and elusive sustenance; this book, and the project developed around it, aim in a small way to help Third World women and those who work on their behalf to give substance to their dream.

Because there has been a high failure rate among women's handicraft projects, development agencies have a responsibility to approach such income-creating programmes more professionally than has been the case in the past. The Women and Development Programme of the Commonwealth Secretariat has therefore developed a programme (funded by the Commonwealth Foundation) which is complementary to this book. It attempts to assist women's bureaux, NGOs and women's groups in a number of Asian and African countries, to identify those handicraft activities which are profitable and those which need changes in order to make them so, and to decide which activities cannot be rescued and should therefore be dropped. It is hoped that a companion study to the current volume will present the findings of this survey.

Dorienne Wilson-Smillie
Adviser to the Secretary General
Women & Development Programme
Commonwealth Secretariat

CHAPTER I

New Jobs for Old

In developing countries throughout the world, rural women are struggling with a problem—a problem which has been aggravated rather than alleviated by the conventional development strategies of recent years. It relates to the need for income—a need which is increasing as traditional barter systems are supplanted by cash economies. It is also a need which women are finding increasingly difficult to satisfy, as their hold on cash income is eroded by their displacement from traditional income-earning activities.

To a large extent, the battles have been fought and won as to if and why women in rural households—as well as men—need access to cash. The struggle to find appropriate and acceptable ways of enabling women to spend their time as productively as possible in support of their families is far from over, however. Anyone interested or involved in programmes aimed at helping rural women to earn increased incomes will be only too well aware of the difficulty of finding ideas, information and guidelines on how best to proceed. It is to them that this book is addressed in the hope that it will provide a source of ideas and inspiration.

As its title suggests, the main focus of the book is on the experiences gained through implementing projects aimed at providing rural women with income, by giving them access to productive village-level employment. Some of these activities, such as baking and other types of food processing, conform with the normally held conception of what constitutes women's work. Others, such as blacksmithy and the construction of roofing sheets, are less likely to fit in with conventional views on the type of work women should, can and do undertake. Female blacksmiths, bakers and roofing-sheet-makers are just three of the many women's occupations reviewed in this study. Together, they provide an interesting picture of the potential for increasing the rate of rural development by increasing women's productivity in the execution of traditional tasks and, where necessary, by enabling them to substitute new jobs for old.

1. WHY DO RURAL WOMEN NEED CASH?

Increasing landlessness in combination with other economic and demographic forces has created a compelling need, in most developing countries, for the expansion of non-agricultural employment in rural areas. Women tend to be particularly vulnerable to displacement from land by commercialization of agriculture, and from traditional income-generating activities by investment in capital-intensive industries. Not surprisingly, the literature on the subject abounds with examples of the adverse impact of modernization on women. One study sums up the situation thus:

> African women who brew beer in their village look forward to the day when a new road will carry their products to the regional centre, only to find to their dismay that the road brings them imported beer instead. Women who smoke and sell fish discover that new refrigerated warehouses and freezer plants undermine their business. Other locally produced foods and condiments give way to factory products. In addition, machine textiles replace handwoven goods; metal and plastic utensils replace earthenware; synthetics replace cotton. The process is intensified by the spread of capital intensive urban based technology that threatens a wide range of cottage industries and artisanal activities that have long provided income for women—handweaving, rice pounding, oil processing. Although the processes outlined affect all workers in small-scale craft and related industries, additional forces work specifically against women. The new heavy industries typically demand male labour while even in light rural industries—except when women are thought to be uniquely suited to certain skills—men often replace women as techniques are upgraded.[1]

[1] R. Dixon, *Jobs for Women in Rural Industry and Services* (Washington, WID, 1979), p. 14.

At the same time, with such basic items as oil, salt, clothes, matches, soap, and even daily food supplies, having to be purchased in the marketplace by rural households, there is an urgent need for rural women to increase, or at least maintain their hold on cash income. There are two major reasons for this. First, the number of households which are headed up by women (i.e. have a woman as their sole means of support) is higher than most people realize and is increasing. The problem is particularly pronounced in parts of Africa where incidences of female-headed households exceed 33 per cent (Kenya, Botswana, Lesotho): the average for sub-Saharan Africa is 22 per cent.[2] But wherever they are found, women-headed households are among the poorest of the poor since they do not now have the same access to land, employment, technology and credit as do those headed by men.

Second, even in male-headed households, it has been found that the interests of the family are often best served if women members have a means of earning and controlling cash incomes of their own. A number of sources examining family consumption patterns have indicated that women express more concern for, and spend more of their income on, the health and feeding of their families than the men, who tend to commit resources to consumer goods, prestige items or entertainment. Hence the incidences of falling standards of child nutrition in households where income levels are going up. A recent study which surveyed available evidence on this issue concluded that 'the evidence, as scattered and unco-ordinated as it is, is strong enough to justify the assumption that enhancing women's contribution to family production and income is a sensible way of ensuring an immediate improvement in the health and welfare of family members.'[3]

2. WHAT IS WRONG WITH HANDICRAFTS?

If, in creating development projects consideration has actually

---

[2] J. Dhamija, Technology as a Threat to the Development of Women's Skills. *Ceres* (1981), Nov/Dec.
[3] N. Nelson, *Productive and Income Generating Activities for Third World Women.* (New York, UNICEF, 1979) p. 19.

The trend should be away from activities which cater for an already overcrowded tourist and export market.

been given to the role and needs of women, it has generally been in the form of a women's 'component' which recognizes, and aims to support, the woman as nurturer and protector of family health and nutritional welfare. Hence the stream of women's projects which are concerned with health and nutrition education, sanitation improvements and child care. Recent evaluations have indicated that as many as two-thirds of specific women's projects funded by major donor agencies, such as USAID, fall into this category.[4]

[4] International Centre for Research on Women, *Limits to Productivity: Improving Women's Access to Technology and Credit* (Washington, AID, 1980).

More recently, there has been a growing awareness that projects of this type are unrealistic in view of the conditions existing in the rural areas of most developing countries. Women simply do not have the time or the money to attend classes, or to put into practice what they have learned. Spurred on by the growing amount of survey data, which reveals that rural women themselves identify a means of earning cash as their major need, interest and funds have at last turned to issues of productivity and earnings.

Unfortunately, much of the initial effort to increase women's earnings has tended to concentrate on the development of crafts, and especially those crafts, such as sewing, basket-making and embroidery, which are normally thought of as being female activities. There are three issues involved here. First, in many countries the 'handicrafts' introduced through women's projects are not those crafts traditionally carried out by women. Therefore, as one researcher puts it, 'shrewd poor women from rural areas who have to select survival strategies often do not wish to participate in these soft options (sewing, knitting, crafts—often unsaleable) as they cannot afford to take risks. Hence, so often they are not co-opted, and it is 'evaluated' that they do not participate in 'income generating' programmes'.[5] This sort of experience stems directly from the mistaken belief that rural women are underemployed and just waiting for someone to teach them how to make pretty but useless items to occupy their time, and bring in a bit of pocket money as well. Nothing, of course, could be further from the truth: a more relevant approach would be to identify which activities rural women are already engaged in and to try to raise productivity of labour so as to increase existing earnings; or to help transform a subsistence activity into an income-generating one.

Second, when attempts are made to introduce improved techniques or technologies aimed at increasing productivity, the result can often be that men take over traditional women's industries. In the same way that the introduction of the plough to men allowed them to monopolize cash crop production, so

[5] D. Jain, *Women's Employment as Related to Rural Areas* (Institute of Social Studies, Delhi, 1980), p. 21.

the introduction to men of many craft improvements has allowed them to monopolize activities which, in many countries, are traditionally women's work. The introduction of kick-wheels into pottery production, and its subsequent domination by men, is an example of this.[6] The fact that women have been excluded has nothing to do with the technology itself, but rather with the assumptions and conditions under which it was introduced. As long as it is assumed that men do blacksmithy, woodworking and pottery, while women do sewing, embroidery, spinning and weaving this trend will continue. Although most societies distinguish between men's crafts and women's crafts, there is in fact no universal rationale in this division of labour. What is unacceptable in one society may be common practice in another. For example, we generally think of blacksmiths as men, but anyone who has travelled by road in Northern India has seen women ironsmiths hammering the metals that are forged into agricultural implements. Similarly, women are supposed to be weavers by tradition, but in most parts of Africa it is the man who weaves.[7]

There are no hard and fast rules about what men's activities are and what women's activities are. The only rule appears to be that when a new technology which brings upgraded skills and higher returns is introduced, the men take over. This, according to some researchers, appears to be due to the conditions existing in rural areas which shape women's demand (rather than need) for new types of technology and credit.

> ... low demand for modern technology and credit by women is a function of several factors, including: lack of information concerning availability of credit or technology; limited opportunity for profitable investments; cultural constraints which restrict women in interacting with male bank officials or extension agents; and women's lack of control over other economic resources, such as

[6] M. Carr, *Appropriate Technology for African Women* (Addis Ababa, ATRCW, 1978).
[7] J. Dhamija, *Women and Handicrafts, Myth and Reality* (New York, Seeds Project, 1981).

In India, women work alongside men in many metal-working industries.

land or other property, that realistically prevents them from demanding their resources. Closing the supply/demand circle, women's lack of control over economic resources and the importance given to their reproductive roles causes suppliers to perceive them as poor investment opportunities. This automatically closes to women the channels necessary for access'.[8]

Third, when attempts have been made to diversify and upgrade skills and develop new markets for women's craft products, in order to raise incomes, efforts have often been unsuccessful or counterproductive because they were aimed at a limited or difficult market. At best, the skill/product has been a new one to the area so that the major damage is that the women's group defaults on a loan and perhaps loses some cash. The donor agency may lose some funds as well. At worst, when the skill is a traditional one, projects may be developed which result in the breaking of links with traditional markets and

[8] ICRW, op. cit. p. 10.

In most of Africa it is men rather than women who engage in weaving.

regular (albeit small) incomes. A well-known instance of this, which had disastrous consequences, concerned the production of bleeding Madras, a checked cotton lunghi material (a type of 'sarong' for men) with running colours, which became a short-lived fashion in the United States.

> Local weavers co-operatives switched to production of this new material, using fugitive dyes, and ignored the traditional market for sarongs used by the local men. Suddenly, the demand for bleeding madras in the US ceased and the co-operatives found themselves with huge stocks and no market. This drove a number of co-operatives into bankruptcy and a large number of weavers to the point of starvation.[9]

It is not the purpose of this book to investigate the strengths, weaknesses and potentials of handicraft projects. Suffice it to say that the evidence available suggests that the potential for increasing incomes of rural women through the

[9] J. Dhamija, 1981, *Women and Handicrafts*, op. cit. p. 10.

narrowly defined handicraft projects of the past seems to be very limited. But having said this, there is obviously a need to suggest viable alternatives.

3. WHAT ARE THE ALTERNATIVES?

A major problem with handicrafts has been their focus on small, fickle, élite markets in urban areas and overseas. Design, organizational and marketing problems have posed many difficulties. Furthermore, local groups involved in production rarely free themselves from dependence on institutional support and often suffer great hardship from fluctuations in demand.

The strategy now popularly suggested as an alternative to handicraft production for élite markets is the involvement of rural women in the production and provision of those basic goods and services which are needed on a regular basis by most local communities, and which increasingly have to be paid for with cash. Women are already traditionally involved in the production and provision of many of these goods and services (e.g. cooking oil, ground spices, soap, petty retail, traditional midwifery), either on a subsistence or sale basis. The need in such cases is to upgrade activities so as to raise output and income and to help village women to become, or remain, competitive with large-scale plants producing similar products.

In many instances, the demand for those products traditionally made by village women is declining as incomes rise. Foods and drinks processed from cereals, homespun cloth and earthenware goods, all have a low income elasticity of demand and are facing competition from 'modern' products, often produced in urban-based factories. Here the challenge is to take existing skills and to adapt them (along with the help of upgraded equipment or scaled-down modern technology) to the manufacture of new products (e.g. bread, whiteware china) which have a high income elasticity of demand. Many of the products, which are currently imported into villages from urban-based factories or from overseas, could be made in the neighbourhood if the appropriate technology, training and other support services were available.

Such a strategy involves two separate but interrelated types of activity. First, there is obviously a need for government policy measures to promote the dispersion and diversification of industrial activity in rural areas. These should include policies to encourage the development of technologies which are appropriate to such industrialization. There is a small, but growing, literature on this subject which indicates that while governments are increasingly stating their interest in rural industrialization, little is happening by way of effective implementation of policies aimed at supporting it.[10,11] Strategies aimed at creating employment in rural areas for men and women depend on rational policy choice and implementation: creation of a large bakery in a city will deprive many rural dwellers of a means of employment in rural bakeries, irrespective of whether the bakers are women or men.

Second, there is a need for grass roots measures to organize employment projects and schemes for rural women in various types of production and service activities aimed at local markets. There is now a growing literature on the experiences involved in implementing projects of this type, although it is not always widely available—much of it being in the form of internal monitoring or evaluation reports prepared by, or for, the implementing agencies. Despite the difficulties involved in obtaining data, there have been a few surveys undertaken at international and national levels, nonetheless. These have been aimed at tabulating the variety of activities found in women's projects and at estimating the numbers of successes and failures in project implementation and the reasons for these.[12,13,14]

By and large, such surveys have shown that the preferred activities are vegetable growing, livestock rearing, poultry rearing, sewing and marketing: in other words, extensions of women's traditional role as food producer and processor—

[10] M. Carr, 'Appropriate Technology and Rural Industrialisation', *ITDG Occasional Paper 1* (London, ITDG, 1982).
[11] S. Sinha, 'Planning for Rural Industrialization,' *ITDG Occasional Paper 8* (London, ITDG, 1983).
[12] N. Nelson, op. cit., pp. 27 and 48.
[13] American Home Economics Association, *Proceedings of Workshop on Income Creation for Rural Women*, (Jamaica, 1981).
[14] N. Simi, *Evaluation of Income Earning Projects by Women in Samoa* (Women's Advisory Committee, Apia, 1983).

Women can make a wide range of commodities, including pottery, which are needed by local communities.

often based on existing skills—rather than the entry of women into the production of a wider range of community goods and services. Predictably, the factors most often cited as constraints on implementation are a lack of training; resentment on the part of husbands or communities; shortage of time; absence of markets; lack of management or organization of project; and no credit facilities. Equally predictably, the major reasons for success tend to be: adequate access to training, markets and credit; good organization and support for activities from men and communities. Suggestions for action which arise from these surveys and studies include the need to understand the position of women in society and their wants; the need for time allocation studies and women's skills inventories; the need for more appropriate technologies; the need for economic surveys of available raw materials and markets; the need to choose an appropriate form of organization, whether co-operative, individual artisan or dispersed factory system; and the need to monitor projects.[15]

A major problem with existing surveys is the lack of detailed

[15] See for example conclusions of N. Nelson, op. cit.

information given on the projects themselves, and on the experiences gained in implementing them. This, combined with the difficulty in gaining direct access to evaluation reports and case studies of individual projects, has resulted in a largely unfulfilled demand from development planners and practitioners for detailed information on the implementation of non-handicraft-oriented income-generating projects involving rural women. In the hope that it goes some way towards meeting such a demand, this book concentrates heavily on the practical details of project implementation. Fifty-five case studies from around the world, which illustrate the successes and shortcomings of women's projects, are presented in Chapter II. Many of the cases are taken from reports of agencies such as the Intermediate Technology Development Group and from other sources, which are not available through normal outlets. For this reason, a list of addresses from which further project information can be obtained is appended.

The case studies relate mainly to the production or provision of basic goods and services, for which there is a local (immediate neighbourhood) market and, as far as possible, they exclude activities such as subsistence agriculture and the production of handicrafts for tourist and export markets. In some instances of course, it is difficult to differentiate. For example, it was not always clear whether a vegetable or livestock project was primarily a subsistence or an income-generating activity. Similarly, it was often difficult to evaluate whether textile and fibre activities were primarily related to basic needs or to export markets. For the main part, however, the projects are about village level production for village level purchase and consumption.

The commodities and services which are needed on an ongoing basis by most rural communities seemed to fall naturally into seven broad categories. These are:

Food, Drink and Tobacco: cooking oil, bread, puffed rice, ground spices, fruit preserves, dehydrated vegetables, coconut sweets, biscuits, pickles, smoked fish, dried fish, banana chips, snackfoods, weaning foods, soft drinks, palmwine, beer, bidi making (a form of very cheap cigarette).

Cloth, Clothing and Fibres: silk spinning, cotton ginning, spinning and weaving, wool spinning and weaving, tie-dye, screen printing, dye making, tanning, tailoring, sewing, knitting, uniforms, rope, mats, blinds, fishing nets.

Building Materials, Housing and Household Goods: lime burning, roofing sheets, bricks, water jars, storage containers, stoves, furniture, mats, pots and pans, water filters, biogas digestors, brooms, leaf plates, charcoal, candles, matches, lamps, irons, soap, salt.

Other Consumer Goods: health equipment, (baby scales, bush ambulances, bandages, solar stills); educational equipment (desks, pencils, paper, chalk, day-care toys); umbrellas, torches, sanitary towels.

Other Productive Activities: market gardening, commercial trees, beekeeping, poultry rearing, goat rearing, rabbit rearing, dairy farming, fish farming.

Services: 'barefoot' doctors, veterinarians, mechanics and agriculturalists, milling, custom hire of crop processing equipment, transport services, repair and maintenance.

Producer Goods: agricultural tools, crop processing equipment, spinning machines, looms, brick moulds, ovens, kick-wheels.

While it was not possible to find case studies about women's involvement in the production of every one of these items, a good selection of examples was located for each of the broad categories with the exception of producer goods, for which no sufficiently detailed material could be found. This does not mean to say that projects involving women in such productive activities do not exist: a more comprehensive search would, hopefully, bring several examples to light.

Within these categories, it seemed appropriate to order the cases according to the type of experience they describe; and most of the cases seemed to fall naturally into one of the four following categories:

Increased productivity of existing work. Many projects were aimed at helping women through the introduction of improved technologies, and by providing supporting services. The objective was to enable them to increase output or to improve the quality of traditional products so that they could remain or become competitive in relation to similar products turned out by capital-intensive factories.

Increased access through co-operatives, credit or technological change to income-generating opportunities which were previously unavailable. In many cases, women are denied existing income-earning opportunities, either because they do not have access to co-operatives and credit, or for socio-cultural reasons which make certain types of activity taboo for women. Several projects were aimed at helping women, either by the introduction of co-operative or credit schemes, or by introducing new technologies which altered the nature of work in such a way as to make it more acceptable to them.

Use of existing skills to produce new products or modified traditional products. In many cases the products traditionally produced by women are no longer wanted by rural communities. They prefer the more modern products, which are imported or made in urban-based factories, using imported materials. Several projects were aimed at helping women to adapt their existing skills, to make new products of a type for which there is a growing demand.

New skills to produce new products, or modified traditional products. Finally, a few projects introduced entirely new skills and types of work to women, in an attempt to help them earn income, through production or provision of needed goods and services.

In the following chapter, the main issues raised by each study are listed case-by-case. There is also a brief summary of general themes and issues of importance at the end of each section. These summaries tend to be descriptive rather than analytical: an analysis of findings is presented in Chapter III. At the end there is also a list of the sources from which the case studies were taken; and the addresses of journals and organizations which will be helpful in any hunt for further information.

CHAPTER II
Options for Earning

1. FOOD, DRINK AND TOBACCO

Every day, in millions of villages in Africa, Asia, Latin America and the islands of the Caribbean and South Pacific, hundreds of tonnes of grains, grain legumes, starchy roots, seeds, fruit and vegetables are processed for sale into a variety of convenient foodstuffs or drinks. The food processing 'industry' which accomplishes this daily task is characterized by its small scale, simple technology and low labour productivity. It forms the basis for gainful employment for millions of rural people around the world—most of them women—working mainly part-time within their own households.

This fits in well, therefore, with women's other commitments and is particularly useful in those countries/cultures where women are faced with the need to earn whilst constrained by limited mobility.

Pressure on this type of industry comes from two sources:

(a) the large-scale modern industrial plant producing similar products, e.g. groundnut oil, palm oil, spices, from similar locally produced raw materials; and
(b) firms of all scales and levels of technology, producing competitive products from largely imported materials, e.g. bread, bottled soft drinks/beer, hard boiled sweets, biscuits.

For those traditional foodstuffs for which there is a high and increasing demand (cooking oil, smoked fish, puffed rice), the level of technology used by household enterprises and other constraints on them (e.g. lack of credit) limits their capacity to resond. Thus the arm of those interested in establishing modern, capital-intensive manufacturing plants, aimed at maximizing output only, is strengthened. For the manufacturers of those foodstuffs with relatively low income elasticities of demand (many cereal-based foodstuffs), the picture is particularly grim, especially given the tendency for governments to offer assistance to small and large industries based on 'modern' products and the frequent inability of women to tap such resources or to share in the benefits of change.[1]

Most of the case studies in this section concern projects and schemes which were initiated to help rural women retain control of the food processing industry, either by increasing productivity in existing foodstuffs, or by giving them access to the training and resources needed for the production of new foodstuffs.

Some, such as fish smoking and gari (cassava) processing in Ghana, and oil processing in Sierra Leone and the Upper Volta, illustrate the development and introduction of improved technologies aimed specifically at helping rural women to raise output and income. Others, such as pappad (a type of bread dough) rolling in India and muri (puffed rice) making in Bangladesh, show how women can be helped to earn more income from existing activities, simply by providing a hitherto missing ingredient, such as institutional support services or credit for working capital. Still others, such as baking in Kenya and Botswana, coconut processing in Bangladesh, fruit and vegetable processing in Honduras, baby food manufacture in India, and banana-chip-making in Papua, New Guinea, show how women have been able to start manufacturing non-traditional food products through assistance with training, credit, co-operative advice, new technology, or marketing assistance.

Fish Smoking in Ghana   Fish smoking is a major activity of rural women along Ghana's coast. It is thought to employ as many as 40,000 women, who take the fish from their husbands, process and then market it. Sometimes, women have difficulty in processing the full catches because of a shortage of firewood and the limited capacity of their smoking ovens. A number of

[1] Symmons, E., 'The Small-scale Rural Food-processing Industry in Northern Nigeria', *Food Research Institute Studies*, Vol. XIV, No. 2, 1975, Stanford University, Stanford, California.

agencies have attempted, therefore, to develop and introduce improved smoking ovens to these fish-mammies.

Of the three improved types of oven tried by the women, one was rejected because of its high cost; another was too complex and changed the nature of the product because insufficient heat was retained in the smoking chamber. A third oven was accepted because of its low cost, improved capacity and the similarity of its operation to the traditional fish-smoking process. The only changes it introduced were the addition of more drying trays and greater fuel-burning efficiency.

The Ghana National Council on Women and Development

Improved ovens like this have helped women in Ghana to increase income from fish-smoking.

assisted some of the women at the village of Kokrobite to acquire the improved oven by granting them loans for its purchase. These loans were quickly repaid because of the profitability of the improved equipment. Unfortunately, however, the introduction of the new ovens meant that the women were able to smoke a greater volume of fish than before and the increased demand for raw material could not be met because there had not been a corresponding improvement in the fishermen's equipment.

This case study shows that even though a technology may be designed with the idea of assisting rural women, they themselves may reject it for legitimate economic or socio-cultural reasons. Further, the type of technology most likely to be accepted is that which closely resembles the traditional method and which has obvious economic benefits in use—even then women will need credit to gain access to such technology. Finally, it demonstrates that there is little point in increasing productivity downstream, if the supply of vital raw material is limited. Either some open unemployment will be caused or potential increases in productivity will not be realized.

Gari Processing in Ghana   Gari (processed cassava) is becoming increasingly popular in Ghana because of the shortage of many other food items and because, once prepared, it is easy to cook. To prepare gari, however, is a very time-consuming, laborious business, which involves peeling and manually grating the fresh cassava, fermenting it over several days, squeezing the water from the fermented cassava and finally, roasting it over a wood fire.

To help women in a village in the Volta Region to increase their income through gari processing, an improved technology was introduced, with the help of the National Council on Women and Development. The process involves a special mechanical grater, a pressing machine to squeeze the water from the grated cassava and a large enamel pan for roasting. This pan holds 10 times the volume of the traditional cassava pot. The system was developed locally, with advice on design from the women themselves.

Before the introduction of this innovation, the women of

the village produced 50 gari bags (weighing 50 kg each) every week. Now they are able to produce 5,000 to 6,000 bags a week. However, this increased output of gari can only be maintained with a higher yield of cassava in the area. Therefore, a male cassava grower's association has been formed to step up cassava production and a tractor has been acquired by the women's co-operative so as to put more land under cassava cultivation.

Involving the women in the design of the new technology undoubtedly contributed to the success of the project. It is interesting that the women obtained the funding to set their men up in a cassava production unit—perhaps men could learn from this example when the bottleneck is with processing capacity!

Oil Processing in Sierra Leone Palm oil production and processing in Sierra Leone is largely carried out by traditional methods. Both men and women are involved. While men harvest the fruit-laden branches, the women's task is to separate manually the fruits from the bunches. Crushing the fruit, by treading, is done by both males and females. It is then the women's job to transport water to wash the crushed fruits. The women then reboil the crude oil to produce pure oil. The demands on women to supply water for processing are considerable. The availability of water is, in fact, the biggest limitation on traditional processing as the peak period of production occurs during the dry season when water is scarce.

Since palm oil processing is an important source of income for rural women, the need to relieve constraints on such processing and increase the productivity of women's labour was identified. Given the tendency for technologies to be designed without consideration of women's requirements and for men to take over these jobs once new technologies have been introduced, an attempt was made to develop a women-oriented project. The aim was to incorporate women's priorities into the design of the press and then to introduce oil presses directly to groups of village women involved in oil processing. Presses were designed by the university to the Ministry of Social Welfare's specification and, with UN funding, a few prototypes were produced for testing in oil-processing villages.

Although the oil presses were installed in 13 villages, it appears that in many of them there was little field testing done. In some cases the villagers simply refused to use the new press; in others, after an initial demonstration, they refused to take part in any further trials. In one instance the press became damaged in use, and was never returned from Freetown, where it had been taken for repair. Proper field testing in other villages was difficult due to a lack of transport to enable demonstration and monitoring. Furthermore, many presses were introduced during the off-peak season.

In those villages where field testing was carried out, results were not favourable. The machine was reported to be too small; there were no time savings; output was actually lower than that obtained with the traditional method; the machine was not easily operated by women and the process used more firewood—a scarce commodity—than before. In total, the new 'improved' press was firmly rejected by the villages in the pilot scheme.

This project, which was designed to incorporate some of the lessons learned from experiences of previous technology and employment projects, ran into just as many difficulties itself. Part of the problem seemed to lie in the lack of communication between social welfare staff and the engineers at the university. The engineers relied entirely on information from social welfare officers. The social welfare officers, however, failed to note or pass on relevant information, because they did not understand its importance for the project. Since the engineers had been told that it would be useful for the equipment to be portable, so that it could be moved between villages, they concentrated on this feature and ignored the more important consideration of the normal batch processing size wanted by the villagers. They also developed an energy-intensive boiler for use in an area of firewood shortage!

Once the prototype had been designed, the university staff were unable to produce the required numbers for testing. Their priorities were to teach and develop new projects, not to manufacture the equipment itself. Most of the presses arrived

One of thirteen oil-presses developed and tested in villages in Sierra Leone.

too late for the main harvest and were delivered to the villages for testing in the off-peak season. Pressure of work and lack of transport also made it difficult for both engineers and social workers to visit test sites, so there was no attempt to modify the prototypes in line with the villagers' responses and reactions.

Even if the prototype had been modified and had proved to be acceptable and useful, no arrangements had been made for scaling up for commercial manufacture and distribution to supply the demand generated. It was obviously not a job for the university and the design was too complicated for the average rural metal-working shop. In any case, producers of metal goods were experiencing enormous problems in acquiring imported raw materials. This is a classic example of how crucial it is to make sufficiently detailed studies of the technical, economic and socio-cultural aspects of the process to be upgraded. It also demonstrates that, before embarking on a project which aims at generating interest in a new piece of hardware, thought needs to be given as to how large numbers could be produced and disseminated.

Oil Processing in Upper Volta Peanuts have never been as important a crop in the north of Upper Volta as they are in the south; and they have traditionally been eaten or sold as a cash crop. However, as milk and butter production have declined in recent years, peanut oil has become more important.

The Save the Children Federation has been working to teach local women how to make peanut oil and, as part of the improvement programme, experiments are being carried out with a variety of improved press types aimed at increasing the efficiency of the oil extraction process. A model developed by a local Voltaic organization seemed to meet the relevant criteria: it was small, low cost, simple to use and locally produced. The press was taken for testing with women's groups in the northern region.

Traditionally, the women produce oil in large quantities. Thirty kilos of peanuts are needed to produce 1.5 litres of oil. Low volume production is inefficient because the time and effort involved is considerable. The preparation process is the same for both the traditional and the new methods. First the nuts are shelled with a decorticator. Then they are grilled over a fire. The skins of the grilled nuts are then removed by using a wood block and a mat made from millet stalks. In the traditional method, the next step is to grind the nuts into a paste. This operation is carried out at the local mill. Boiling water is then stirred into the paste. Little effort is needed for this, although it does require fuel. The oil rises to the surface and is skimmed off as the mixture is stirred. When using the new oil press, the peanuts are chopped finely or pounded in the water. This takes much longer, but the milling process is eliminated and thus the small mill fee is not paid.

Using the traditional method it was possible to produce half a litre of oil in half an hour, whereas it took two hours to produce the same quantity from the oil press. In addition, the type of press used created several problems, only some of which could be rectified easily. The pressing plate repeatedly jammed inside the cylinder; the press itself was only large enough to handle about 2 kg of nuts at a time (not enough to make it worth the effort); it cost more than traditional equipment; and was heavy, hard to clean and totally unfamiliar to the women.

Finally, although the new press eliminated the skimming operation, this is, in fact, one of the easier steps in the whole process. It would have made more sense to develop a mechanical process to handle the slow, laborious task of removing the skin from the grilled nuts. In the traditional method of processing, women make a bigger profit by selling the by-product, Kuli-Kuli's (peanut cookies) than by selling the oil itself. However, the by-product from the oil press is a hard, cake-like mass of chopped nuts that can be used as animal food or pounded into powder for cooking sauces, but the marketability of this product is dubious.

It was decided that if oil production was to become a viable activity in the area, funding should be used to buy peanut decorticators and/or grain mills rather than oil presses. These could be used on a co-operative basis in the villages as part of a credit and training programme.

This study illustrates the danger of designing a machine for women without consultation or investigation into existing practices. Furthermore, it should never be assumed that because something is small it is automatically appropriate for small producers: it can be so small as to be useless. Technology which allows co-operative ownership, or at least fair access to a larger-scale technology, may make much better sense economically.

Coconut Sweets in Guyana Following a ban on the import of cakes, biscuits and sweets, there is great demand for such items in most parts of Guyana. Coconuts grow in abundance in the coastal areas and traditionally shredded coconut has formed the basis for many types of confectionery. The National Women's Party thus saw the making of coconut sweets as a potentially viable income-generating venture for women's groups around the country.

The idea appealed because it used existing skills and there was a large, potential market for such products. But the women were quick to point out that the traditional process of grating fresh coconuts, using a perforated tin, was an extremely laborious and time-consuming task. The work was unpleasant and productivity was low. The process would act as a constraint to the commercial production of confectionery.

The women's movement approached a small manufacturing company in Georgetown which was known to be involved in the design and production of small-scale agricultural equipment. The problem was explained to the manager: was it possible to develop a small, simple, manually operated low-cost coconut grinder to improve on traditional technology? Development work commenced and the first prototypes were soon ready. These were taken by representatives of the women's movement for demonstration and testing to groups around the country. They were also demonstrated by staff members attending conferences in other parts of the Caribbean. Wherever they went, the graters were an immediate success. Enquiries began to filter through.

Herein lay a problem. The manufacturers had only made 12 graters. Expanding into commercial production was going to entail considerable investment and would not be worthwhile unless orders of several thousands could be guaranteed. The manager was not convinced that a sufficiently large market existed, especially since the intended users were poor women, who certainly wanted the new grater, but did not necessarily have the cash to buy one. The women's movement began to investigate a likely source of funding to finance the volume order necessary. The graters could then be sold on to women's groups through various channels. In the meantime, they also urged the manufacturer to try to adapt the grater so as to make it even cheaper. This was done by substituting readily available wood for some of the metal parts. Funds were located, an order for 5,000 graters was placed, and commercial production commenced.

Some of these graters now form the basis of successful enterprises making locally sold coconut sweets. Initiative has not stopped there, however. The women's organization is now establishing productive women's enterprises using other parts of the coconut, such as the shell and the fibres, to make other locally demanded commodities. For example, some women have been shown how to make buttons from the shell, while others are making mattresses from the fibre. Assistance has now been sought from the local technology institution in upgrading the fibre processing techniques so that higher value products, such as mats and rope, can be made from this.

Of the 5,000 graters made 1,100 were distributed to women's groups throughout the coconut growing areas of Guyana. A few have reached women in other parts of the Caribbean through the 'women in development' network. It seems only a matter of time, however, before the normal commercial channels take up distribution in the islands. A Dominican businessman has already approached the women's movement and the manufacturer to negotiate sales and distribution rights.

The case study shows how small enterprises based on local raw materials can often flourish as a result of bans on imported consumer goods. The way in which the women's organization, having identified market opportunities, set about facilitating the design, development, production and marketing of a needed technology is noteworthy. Agencies dealing with women's projects do not always know how to do this; at the same time universities and commercial firms are unlikely to initiate and push through technological developments which have low prestige and where markets are uncertain.

Corn and Cheese Biscuits in Honduras   In the village of Esquimay (population 1,000), in impoverished South Honduras, a group of local women came to Save the Children Federation/ Community Development Foundation (CDF), which was currently working in the area, to seek assistance for their own project. They explained that the primary source of income in

Esquimay was the sale of rosquillas, a hard biscuit made from corn and cheese. Grinding corn was a long, laborious job, so time-consuming that the women were never able to produce enough to make as many rosquillas as they could sell.

At the suggestion of CDF, the women's group organized a meeting with the whole community—men and women—to consider whether an integrated community-based programme would be feasible and of interest. Since it was, CDF suggested the formation of a community committee. Although there was some resistance on the part of the men towards the participation of women in the meetings it was, after all, the women who had brought in agency assistance. The committee was thus duly organized with 40 women and 20 men. The leader of the women's group was elected secretary. After talks with community leaders, it was decided that a motor-driven corn mill, which would increase production of corn meal and reduce women's labour, would be the most beneficial first project for the community. The agency donated the down payment for the corn mill and made a loan to the community committee for the first payment. Each woman paid a small sum for the use of the mill and from the profits earned by the mill the loan was repaid. Rosquilla production and sales increased.

Encouraged by their success, the women decided to form a baking co-operative to produce rosquillas more efficiently. Although the co-operative started well, it was soon apparent that the women preferred to work in their own homes—whether for reasons of individual differences or family demands. The mill, however, continues to serve the community and the women appreciate their additional income and time.

Spices and Pickles in Bangladesh A large indigenous non-governmental organization (NGO) in Bangladesh has helped thousands of landless women through the group production of a variety of basic foodstuffs and other goods. One project involves assistance to a group of rural women in the production and marketing of a range of ground spices, pickles and sauces.

The spices are of a high quality and, in this respect, compare favourably with other packaged brands on the market, most of which are adulterated. However, their purity means that prices are higher than those of their competitors.

This was a problem initially but it is now felt that the brand is becoming known for quality. Sales rose from TK 3,000 per month to TK 5,000 per month in a six-month period. The stone-grinding method is very time consuming, but the group was helped to increase the productivity of its labour by the introduction of a simple hand-operated grinding mill, imported from the UK. The loan on this is being repaid from sales of spices. In future, other mills will be made by a local engineering firm to the British design.

A less successful product is a high-sugar vegetable pickle. Spoilage problems were very common. An independent evaluator of the project found that the fault lay largely with the pickle formulation. The bottle and cans used were also totally inadequate. If the bottle was inverted the cap or lid would fall off. The conclusion was that the agency responsible for the project did not have the technical base to enter food manufacturing activities of this type.

Obviously, involvement in food processing of certain kinds requires a good understanding of technology. If skills do not

Bangladeshi women preparing foods for preservation.

already exist within a group and the agency involved in the project does not have an in-house food technologist or good access to technical advice, then more complicated processing should be avoided.

Pappad Rolling in India Shri Makila Gricha Udyog Lijjat Pappad is a women's food processing co-operative with over 6,000 active, earning members. During 1978-79 the organization manufactured and sold Lijjat Pappad, worth Rs 3 crores, through its 21 branches, throughout India. This was a remarkable achievement for the seven lower-income group women who first thought up the idea in 1959.

The originators borrowed Rs 80 to get started and paid this back with interest within six months. The institution opted for the goal of self-reliance and self-growth from the start and as a matter of principle no monetary help or donation was to be sought from any source. As such, the work started on a sound commercial footing as a small-scale venture. This, together with the principle of maintaining a very high quality product, has contributed to the organization's success.

Lijjat is unique as an organizational model. It is a women's organization, a public trust, a registered society and a co-operative. It is a commercial enterprise which manufactures and sells selected goods. Legally, Lijjat is registered simultaneously under the Societies Registration Act and the Public Trust Act in Bombay. But functionally, it has incorporated all the features of a co-operative society. Operationally, it has organized its business activity in a manner generally associated with commercial enterprises. Any woman above the age of 15 can become a member/co-owner of the Lijjat organization—the only other condition of entry being the signing of a pledge whereby she agrees to certain principles, such as religious devotion to work, co-operation for the maximum benefit of all members, rolling of pappads for Lijjat only, rolling a minimum of 3 kg of dough each day, and the subordination of self-interest to the larger interest of the Lijjat organization at all times. As the members are spread throughout seven Indian states, the incorporation of a pledge to some ethical system has been essential to the cohesion of the organization.

Lijjat can probably best be described as a modification on the put-out or dispersed factory system of production; one in which the normal disadvantages are reduced, if not removed.

For women who are still not able to leave their homes for long hours and thus prefer work which can be done at home, Lijjat offers a way of doing this without the women having to endure exploitation or domination. In Lijjat, all the intermediaries are women and all are members. All workers are partners rather than employees.

The day for a Lijjat centre begins very early in the morning. The supervisor, normally risen from the ranks of the pappad rollers, has already prepared flour and spices the day before. At about 4 am, the women engaged in the preparation of the dough arrive at the centre and start work. Most centres have their own mini-buses which collect staff from home. By 6 am the dough is ready for distribution to members, who bring with them the pappads they have prepared at home the day before. The pappads are weighed. The receivers tally the quantity of dough taken in the previous morning. Quality control checks are very thorough and very strict; if the pappads are not clean, white and completely dried, they are rejected. They are then sent to the packing section for packing in polyethylene bags and labelling. Members are paid according to quantity and quality, and given the next consignment of dough. This will be rolled out at home in the afternoon, after the women have done their household tasks and when the sun is very hot, so that the pappads dry quickly. On an average, payment amounts to about Rs 7.20 for 6 kg of pappad with Rs 1.20 deposited in the compulsory savings account. A woman can earn anything between Rs 4 and Rs 40 per day.

Production is never carried out on the co-operative premises. In the case of rural centres such as that of Valod in Gujarat, this necessitates some positive adaptation of the system since members' homes do not have the space or are not clean enough for food processing. Here, the organization provides the women with sheds to work in. It is also considering extending into products such as matches, agarbattis (incense sticks) and leather goods to overcome this constraint and enable rural groups to set up more centres, thus creating more jobs in these areas.

In a pragmatic departure from the accepted practice of co-operative endeavours, which rely on official marketing outlets (e.g. Khadi Village Industry Commission (KVIC)), or on other semi-official organizations, Lijjat adopted strictly commercial marketing techniques from the very beginning. It appointed agents on a commission basis, ensuring that only those who had previously enjoyed a reputation for successful business dealings were selected. By offering a commission per packet sold, the Lijjat organizers involved the agents directly in the sale of pappads, and created conditions in which maximum sales would be ensured. This deliberate choice of a commercial marketing network reflects the instinctive commercial orientation of the Lohana community which founded the Lijjat enterprise.

The Lijjat model shows how women can work at home on a put-out basis without the exploitation element so common elsewhere in India. It also shows how this non-exploitative approach does not necessarily mean a non-commercial one. Every attempt is made to maximize profits through normal commercial means but all workers are members and all share in the profits.

Puffed Rice in Bangladesh In Bangladesh, many agencies are involved in giving individual landless women very small loans which is normally all that is required to embark on a household-level rice processing business. Equipment costs are low in such activities, with mainly household items used, but the working capital needed to purchase unprocessed paddy is often beyond the means of very poor families. Loans to overcome this problem can therefore help to provide employment for many women using existing skills and equipment.

One common rice processing activity supported by such loans is the production of muri (puffed rice). Both men and women engage in this activity, the men in transportation and marketing and the women on the skilled production side. Paddy is purchased in the local market and taken to the farmsteads where the women parboil it twice and dry it. The men take it to the local rice mill, for milling, and then return it to the farmsteads where the women separate the grain from the mixed bran and husk. Although the mill delivers rice from one outlet, and bran/husk from another, the men normally load all of this into one bag which the women then have to painstakingly separate out again, using a winnowing tray. The chaff, with dried leaves, is used for fuel in parboiling paddy and puffing rice. Puffing demands great skill to ensure that the final product is as white as possible, since this is the premium grade. The finished product is then either sold locally or taken by bus to the major wholesale market in Dhaka. In either case, it is the men who transport and sell the final product and control the earnings.

A Bakery in Kenya The women of Bomani Village in Kenya decided to set up a bakery. They earned the money to get started by selling their traditional handicrafts (baskets and weaving). Help was hired to build a big brick oven. Two members of the group went on a bread-baking course and came back and taught the others basic bread-baking techniques. The women elected a treasurer, pooled their money to buy supplies, worked out a schedule for sharing the baking and planned how to distribute the bread.

The bakery turned out to be far more than an activity in economic development. Health, nutrition, sanitation, family life, business skills, co-operation between men and women, and leadership in the village, were all affected by the women's project.

First of all, the bakery had to be built according to government specifications. A latrine was required by law. The Ministry of Health set standards of cleanliness for workers to follow. The workers, themselves, had to be immunized against certain diseases.

The men were impressed by the women's achievement and many of them began to help. Some did so by allowing their wives to come to learning sessions. Others contributed money or labour. The women learnt how to keep records, manage their money, and use the services of a bank. Many are now learning to read and write and to use more sophisticated mathematics in accounting for their income and expenses. They have also learned that they are capable of carrying out an activity that is important to their community; that they can deal with the authorities that provide access to the resources they need for further activities; and that they have justifiable confidence in their considerable abilities.

The original concept has grown to include a second oven, a bakery building, and a tea and bread kiosk. The women are marketing their bread in other villages. They are now talking about starting a poultry project to provide eggs for the bakery and an additional source of income and food.

The undertaking has not been an easy one. Raising the money to fund the bakery was difficult. The group met weekly, and there were constant problems with those who arrived late or failed to attend. The women were strict about their agreements, however, and stern with those who failed to abide by them. They often charged a fine for absences. The latrine shed fell down while the women were building it and they had to start again. There were early problems with the bread, and the two women who had originally learned to make it had to go back to the training centre to re-learn how to measure ingredients.

But the women persevered and the project began to prosper. They decided to keep their money in the bank, rather than at the treasurer's home, so that it would earn interest. Today the group's bread is much in demand. The group, itself, has gained a lot more than a way to earn some money.

A Bakery in Botswana The Roman Catholic Mission in Serowe runs training courses for women who are unable to go on to secondary school, either because they do not have the necessary grades, or because of a shortage of money in the family. One of the courses run by the Mission is cooking/baking. Surplus produce from these courses used to be sold to the villagers. Out of this evolved the idea of building a bakery and employing some of the ex-trainees from the school.

Funds were obtained from the US Embassy's small projects fund, premises were built and an International Voluntary Service volunteer with baking and management skills was recruited to manage the bakery and to train at least two women in practical management.

Initially, all went well. Women were trained in the necessary management and accounting skills, and the produce from the bakery—bread, meat pies, scones—was sold in local village stores. In an eight-month period sales increased five fold. Small retailers came to the bakery and placed orders and even collected them by vehicle, daily. Bread was delivered to nearby stores by hand. The wages of the 10 women employees went up from 36 pula per month to 66 pula per month in this period.

Difficulties arose in meeting demand mainly because of the small oven, which only had a 40-loaf capacity, and because the premises were too cramped and not designed for the purpose for which they were being used. The 'volunteer' manager had also had no success in persuading the women to form themselves into a producers' co-operative to run the bakery. They had no idea what a co-operative was and preferred to be employed; they saw the mission as their employer. While the women were efficient in their work, promoting the idea that they should be making their own decisions was difficult.

Because there was no electricity in the area, a small industrial oven using cylinders of gas and a large gas refrigerator, were installed. Apart from this equipment, there are no machines, although there is a solar panel for hot water which has proved useful for dough-making, washing up, and other activities. Another drawback is the remoteness of the area. This means that supplies from the local wholesaler are quite expensive, due partly to his monopoly position, and partly to transport costs.

After about 14 months operation, bread sales dropped by 60 per cent in less than a week. Over the next few months they continued to decline. It appears that this was due to a decision of the large bakery in Gaberone (370 km to the south) to expand production and to sell bread throughout the eastern side of Botswana. Consumers switched to this bread because it was slightly cheaper, as the larger bakery bought flour direct from the flour mill in Pretoria whereas the Serowe bakery obtained it through two wholesalers who each took their 'cut'; it was mechanically wrapped, which made it look more attractive than the Serowe bread, manually wrapped in cheap plastic bags; it was delivered direct to customers; and it had a shelf life of five days as opposed to two days for the Serowe bread.

Before leaving Botswana, the volunteer manager asked the local council to support local industry by buying bread from the Serowe bakery for hospitals, prisons and other institutions. This has allowed production to continue, but it is uncertain how long the contract will last.

Solar-dried Coconut in Bangladesh Noakhali District is one of the poorer areas of Bangladesh which, although very fertile, is very densely populated and has a high incidence of landlessness. Many agencies are involved in job creation programmes for landless families.

One agency, Menonite Central Committee (MCC), decided to provide long-term jobs to landless women by introducing them to the technique of solar drying. After experimentation, it was found that the technique could be successfully applied to the drying of locally available foodstuffs, some of which could well be commercially viable. Coconut was chosen as having the best potential, however, because it makes a fine, clean product acceptable to a variety of markets. Furthermore, the reduction in weight, through husking and drying, is substantial. This is important since coconut is only grown in certain areas of Bangladesh and transportation is expensive.

Women were selected from needy families and trained in the production and use of solar dryers. The project was set up as a producers' association approved under the umbrella of MCC's registration with the Department of Social Welfare. A manager was hired by the project and he reports to a government official and an MCC official. At the moment, the women have difficulty in thinking of themselves as owners of the project, but hopefully a committee will evolve, giving the producers full control. The number of women involved has risen from 12 in 1980, to 60 in 1983.

The project produces solar-dried coconut powder. The product is 100 per cent pure and no oil is removed. Coconuts are purchased in bulk from local coconut growers. The women clean, grate and sulphur (to preserve) the coconut. It is then

One of the stages in the village-level production of dried coconut powder in Bangladesh.

dried to 4 per cent moisture in solar dryers which the women build themselves at a cost of less than TK 200 per unit. The producers are paid on a piece-rate basis and their earnings average TK 250 to TK 300 per month. They can dry the coconuts in their own homes on a part-time basis. Average production is now 900 kg per month of dried coconut, equivalent to 8,000 whole coconuts.

The women generally buy their coconuts from the project (in 1981 the cost was TK 3 each). They are also free to buy from outside sources. In turn, the project buys dried coconut from the producers at the rate of TK 36.50 per kg. If the producer is careful, 1 kg of coconut powder can be produced from 8.5 coconuts, although the costing is based on a yield of 1 kg per 10 coconuts. The women bring their completed product to the project office where quality and moisture content is checked. Packaging is done in bulk in 25 lb (11.25 kg) polythene bags, as well as in 1 lb (0.45 kg) bags and 9 oz (0.25 kg) packages. The bags are heat sealed and packed in metal drums until shipping time. Shipment is made on foot, by rickshaw, bus, MCC vehicle, or any other practical means.

Ignorance of hygiene procedures, over-sulphuring, and deterioration of packaging due to the high oil content of the coconut and/or low grade plastics have all caused production problems. The biggest difficulty has been to develop sufficient markets to keep all the workers employed. Initially, market studies conducted by MCC showed good acceptance of the grated coconut for home consumption. It was on the basis of this research result that the project was launched. Packaging was in 95 gram plastic bags with a simple plastic label. Many urban shops were contacted, credit sales were given, and it was assumed that only more advertising was needed to make the product take off. However, few shops placed second orders, fewer still made payments, and many complained that the packages were getting dirty, torn and infested with bugs.

The second phase in marketing coconuts was the development of a nicely designed cardboard box which contained 95g bags of coconut, and was itself wrapped with cellophane. This product, again aimed at the retail market, was given advertising support in cinemas and newspapers, but in general people preferred to continue using fresh coconut for home consumption.

The third, and most active phase, occurred when it was discovered that bakers, confectioners and especially biscuit manufacturers preferred the project's coconut. In fact, some began to use this instead of imported Malaysian coconut. Sales, which are mainly carried out through the MCC Marketing Wholesale Centre in Dhaka, are now averaging TK 25,000 per month.

Not surprisingly, the husks and shells of the coconuts from this project have been piling up at an alarming rate. Thus, the intention is to help existing project members and other women in the area supplement their income through coir-making and high-grade charcoal production using these by-products. The decortification of coir fibres by hand is a difficult and energy-consuming task. The MCC has placed an order with a Dhaka engineering firm to produce a husk-rolling machine and a decortifier/stripping machine which will be tested out within the existing project. Little attention seems to have been given, as yet, to markets for coir products. Markets for charcoal made from coconut shells have been investigated: local market prices appear to be very low because, as yet, no suitable design of stove is available for burning this type of fuel. If such a stove could be designed and produced, evidence suggests that there would be a good demand for coconut shell charcoal by specialist tradespeople and craftsmen such as goldsmiths.

Mango Purée in Honduras A group of village women from San Juan Bosco in Honduras approached the Save the Children Federation about ways of making use of the abundant crop of mangoes, many of which were going to waste during the short period they were in season. A feasibility study was carried out, and a project started, to help the villagers form a co-operative to produce and can the purée.

The first year's production of mango purée was all sold, but the second year's sales dropped to half the production run. The following year, the group produced none because they had so much left over from the previous year. Furthermore, there were almost no mangoes that season, as mango trees in that area 'rest' every seven years and produce no fruit.

Obviously, some new initiatives were necessary to revitalize the project. In examining the reasons why the purée was not selling, the group identified three causes: the jars were probably too large, and people tended to buy only as much as they would eat in one day; the glass jars themselves were expensive, thereby raising the cost of the finished product; finally, mango purée is not a traditional Honduran food.

The co-operative members attacked their marketing problems by studying product diversification at a nearby agricultural school. Through this, they learned new methods of preparing and processing various mango and papaya products. They also took courses on the processing of fruit products in vacuum-packed plastic bags. These offered the most interesting possibilities for the project. In addition, they learned about fruit tree planting and grafting. Subsequently, with the help of a special grant from a bilateral donor agency, they planted about 700 mango and papaya trees, which provided them with improved varieties of fruit.

The next step was to gain legal status from the Government. This was achieved only after great effort by the women, but it enabled them to apply for bank loans. They have now diversified their product range to include jams and candy, and have experimented with different packaging materials and types. More recently, they devised a biscuit cone that is filled with mango purée and sells for a few pesos. This has become very popular in the village and in neighbouring areas, and has given the project an important boost. The women are also planning a food co-operative that could operate in their factory during the non-harvest months. This could provide villagers with less expensive foodstuffs, and give members an opportunity to earn income throughout the year and not just at the fruit season.

In a meeting with agency staff, the women discussed the effect of the project on their lives. They believe that it enabled them to provide better food, clothing and medicine for their children and had earned them respect from their families and communities.

Although a feasibility study was undertaken prior to starting production, this was purely technical and ignored such factors as resource base, markets, local incomes and tastes. The way the women have been able to gain access to training and become proficient to the extent of innovating with packaging is interesting, but it should be noted that not all women would be able or allowed to undertake such lengthy training.

Fruit and Vegetable Preserving in Honduras. In a small village in Honduras, 20 women are involved in a business bottling vegetables and fruits, which they started with the help of a US$1,000 loan from UNICEF. This is one of 60 women's clubs in the region which, with UNICEF assistance, is now able to bring in additional family income.

The women have a vegetable garden where they grow onions, maize and beetroot. The rest of their raw materials they buy from local farmers including their own husbands. Before the project began, nobody knew how to preserve vegetables and there was a lot of wastage. With the low interest loan, the women bought pots, bottles, lids, knives and kitchen equipment and established production under the supervision of Ministry of Agriculture staff, who taught them production processes and quality control techniques.

The women had a problem finding a suitable building from which to operate because government officials were very concerned with details, such as the need for a cement floor. At the beginning, the women did not understand the importance of hygiene. But after a training course where they also learned the methods of preservation, they were very concerned to maintain high standards of product quality and hygiene.

The main product of the bottling business is onions—the crop grown most commonly in the area. After only a few months, production went up to 2,000 bottles. A third of the profit from sales was used to pay back the loan. In most cases, the amount the family retains doubles their income.

As a complementary project, the Ministry of Agriculture is assisting local farmers to diversify their crops. This will also mean a diversified product range for the bottling business.

Ready-to-Eat Infant Food Mix in India. A home science college near Madras developed a low-cost, indigenous baby food, using cheaper, locally available foodstuffs. Care was taken to ensure that the technology involved in the infant food mix preparation was simple, thus making it viable for adoption by rural women. Except for grinding the coarse cereal into a fine flour in a mill, all the other operations, such as cleaning the ingredients, winnowing, pounding, sieving, roasting and mixing could be done using manual labour. After mixing the flours in the correct proportions, the ready-to-eat food is hygienically packed in Polyethylene envelopes, sealed and suitably labelled.

A demonstration arranged for the members of women's clubs in selected villages in Tamil Nadu on the preparation and use of the product kindled the interest of one club to venture into production on a commercial basis. A production unit was set up with a capital investment of Rs 1,000, contributed as a loan by the Social Service Association of the Home Science College. Necessary permission, and a licence for the preparation of the product, were obtained for the group from the local government authorities concerned.

Various agencies were approached for help in marketing the food mix. A demonstration-cum-sales campaign was conducted at the co-operative supermarket in Coimbatore to test public response. The product was also exhibited at a World Vegetarian Congress in Madras, and stalls were set up at various trade fairs in the neighbourhood. The response was good, owing to the low cost, taste and high quality of the product. The fact that it was patented by the home science college, well-known in the area, also helped to capture attention and gain acceptance.

Paediatricians were approached to obtain their endorsement for the product as an appropriate food for malnourished infants and children. Nursery schools and residential schools in the area were also approached. After a while, several orphanages and schools were regularly ordering supplies of the food mix, thus offering continuing financial support to the group manufacturing the product.

Palmwine in Nigeria Palmwine, prepared from the white sugary liquid tapped from the base of the young flower of a mature oil-palm tree, is the source of employment for thousands of men and women in Nigeria and other parts of West Africa.

While still a firmly established favourite, because of its low cost in comparison to foreign alcoholic drinks, and because of its reputed medicinal qualities, there is always the danger that palmwine, as it is traditionally prepared and presented could start to lose ground as incomes rise and consumer preferences change in favour of things modern.

In order to protect the local industry and the people employed in it, several Nigerian institutes have pumped thousands of Naira into researching ways of improving the quality and marketability of the product. One major breakthrough has been the glass bottling of palmwine which keeps it fresh for about a year. Normally palmwine, is traditionally presented in a variety of containers—the calabash, for example which has poor protective qualities—and it has to be consumed immediately after purchase.

This represents an interesting example of forward thinking

in respect of planning to safeguard a traditional industry from modern competitive products. Care will obviously need to be taken to ensure that women continue to be involved in making, transporting and marketing the bottled palmwine.

Banana Chips in Papua New Guinea The women in Situm village in Morobe Province had heard that a technology centre at the university in the nearest town could assist communities to start income-generating projects. At their request, a team from the technology centre visited the village to see what could be done.

There was an abundance of bananas in the area, most of which were wasted. Thus the idea arose of starting a village industry based on the processing of bananas into a tasty snack food. The centre's food technologist suggested making the bananas into banana chips—a popular snack food in many parts of South East Asia. This was considered a good idea and so training commenced in processing methods, which include slicing, drying, deep frying and packaging.

The problem arose as to how to accommodate and finance a business based on the new skills. A small loan was given to help purchase or make equipment; the villagers themselves, contributed their labour to make an extension to the community store so production could be carried out there. After two years work, the women have become proficient in banana chip making and the business is flourishing. The men in the village have been very supportive and are actively involved in the community industry too. The outflow of young men to the towns has slowed down because they feel they now have useful work at home: this pleases the women!

There have been many difficulties which could not have been easily overcome without assistance from the technology centre. Apart from the obvious problems involved in learning the process itself, the kerosene stove, used for frying the chips, was found to be very expensive. The technology centre showed the villagers how to build a lorena wood-burning stove (a high-mass mud stove) to replace this, and thus cut costs. The health authorities visited the factory, and were about to close it down, because it did not meet with regulations. The technology

Before they are deep-fried, sliced bananas are laid out on trays to dry.

centre intervened and showed the women how to modify their equipment and handling procedures so that their factory would comply with health regulations. The women were taught how important it was to not handle the finished chips, to keep animals and insects away from foodstuffs and to refrain from smoking. Washing and drainage facilities were also installed. Finally, the technology centre helped to establish a market for the product. First, chips were sold in snack packs on the university campus. These were a great success with staff and students. Second, local supermarkets were also approached and trial orders sold out so quickly that store-keepers wanted to buy far more than the village industry could produce—even if the community were to work full-time, which they prefer not to do.

The economics of the project have yet to be worked out. The setting of a selling price is arbitrary, although the villagers seem happy enough with the return they receive. There has as yet been no repayment on the loan, although this is desired so that a revolving fund can be established to assist other groups establish similar village-based industries elsewhere.

Summary There are a number of themes which recur in income-generating projects for women in the food processing sector.

First, the low level of technology used in traditional processing of food, means that identification, design, development and dissemination of appropriate 'improved' technologies play a major role in food processing projects. While such interventions can be enormously beneficial if successful, the process is fraught with difficulties, and far more thought obviously needs to be given to the means by which technologists, social scientists, community development workers and rural women and men can work together more effectively.

Second, questions of hygiene and packaging become much more important when food processing enterprises move into 'modern' products and when urban markets are being sought.

Third, while traditional food processing industries are carried out very much on an individual basis, most projects seem to require group action/co-operation if they are to operate successfully. To a large extent this is because higher levels of investment are involved, requiring a pooling of resources. It should be noted, however, that in some countries and cultures, women are not willing or able to work in groups.

Finally, government policies can play an important role in food processing industries, either by banning imports of food products (positive effect), or agreeing to the establishment of large-scale plants (negative effect).

2. CLOTH, CLOTHING AND FIBRES

After food processing, cloth-making is the second most important industry for the employment of rural women in basic goods production. It encompasses the operations of ginning, spinning, weaving, dyeing, printing and sewing.

In Africa, most cloth is imported, so textile activities tend to be limited to dyeing, printing and sewing. In areas where cotton is available in limited quantities, rural women tend to gin and spin small amounts for home use. Weaving, using imported yarn, is common in parts of West Africa, but is traditionally a man's work. In the hill countries of the South, spinning local mohair provides an important source of income for rural women, but the end-product is almost totally exported.

In Asia, because of the larger quantities of cotton, wool and fibres, spinning and weaving activities are much more widespread and provide part-time employment for millions of rural women. Sericulture and ericulture are also more widespread in Asia.

As with food processing, village and cottage industries based on spinning, weaving and dyeing are characterized by low-level technology and very low returns to labour. Recent studies of the cloth dyeing industry in West Africa reveal that although there is a strong local demand for gara-dyed (tie and dye) cloth (income elasticity of demand of + 1.4), the hundreds of small production units, predominantly owned and staffed by women, are facing difficulties in expanding output because of constraints on management, production and marketing.[2] Other studies in Asia record the labour-displacing effect of mechanization in the cotton spinning industry, and of the introduction of power looms.[3] In comparison with these, the traditional techniques used by rural women are hopelessly inefficient.

Many of the case studies in this section concern projects aimed at assisting women to maintain or strengthen their position in these textile processes, through the acquisition and control of new techniques and technologies. These include wool and muslin spinning in India, tie-dye in Tanzania, Gambia and Mali, and carpet weaving in Iran. Other studies show how women's incomes from textile processes are increased through improved access to credit (cotton spinning in Upper Volta); breaking of sex-stereotyping (broadloom weaving in Ghana); or the introduction of new fibres and processes (ericulture in Bangladesh).

Several projects relate to tailoring and sewing (tailoring co-

[2] Chuta, E., 'The Economics of the Gara (Tie-Dye) Cloth Industry in Sierra Leone, African Rural Economy Program', *Working Paper No. 25*, Department of Agricultural Economics, Michigan State University, East Lansing, Michigan.
[3] Jain, D., *Women's Employment as Related to Rural Areas* (Institute of Social Studies, Delhi, 1980).

operatives in Tanzania, textiles in Swaziland and school uniforms in Botswana). By and large, these confirm that while such projects are popular in women's programmes, their value is limited, unless products are firmly linked to strong, local markets such as school or government uniforms.

The remaining activity in this category is the processing of fibres or twines (jute, sisal, coconut, synthetic) to make community goods, such as fishing nets, ropes and mats. Again, the technology is very low level and women are often exploited by private traders, both with raw materials and finished product. Two of the case studies—fishing nets in India and rope-making in Sri Lanka—look at projects which have sought to increase women's incomes by eliminating the middlemen and introducing new technologies.

Wool Spinning in India A project was initiated in the remote hill districts of Uttar Pradesh, aimed at increasing the returns from spinning through the development and introduction of an improved hand-spinning device.

Woollen textile production is an important economic activity in the Kumaon region. It is a cottage industry, which takes two forms: one of independent production amongst the Bhotia (scheduled tribe) community, the other of a put-out system, among predominantly cultivating households, controlled by a number of Khadi (home-spun material, literally) organizations under the guidance of the Khadi and Village Industries Commission (KVIC).

In the Bhotia households, woollen textile production is an important source of income—representing from 35 to 70 per cent of total income. Limited involvement in agriculture and a fairly equitable division of labour allow Bhotia women considerable time for their traditional work in woollen textile production. In the average extended family, combined labour input of 8 to 12 hours a day for ten months of the year is possible. The average household in independent production produces six carpets and eleven shawls each year, earning Rs 2,200—far below the official subsistence level of Rs 3,500. With increasing problems related to the availability of wool and ease of access to alternative employment opportunities, woollen textile production amongst Bhotias has declined during the 1970s.

In non-Bhotia households, which are engaged in woollen textile production on a put-out basis, spinning and knitting contribute just 6 per cent of the incomes of the poorer households, and less than 5 per cent of the earnings of the better-off. Woollen textiles production is mostly a part-time occupation for women. Male participation is occasional and entirely casual. Spinning is done mainly with a traditional spinning wheel. A rigid division of labour imposes an enormous burden of domestic and agricultural work on women. This limits the time available for woollen textile production in cultivating households. The spare time available varies according to the season and the number of women in the household who share in the daily chores. Average time devoted annually to woollen textiles in a cultivating household is 375 hours. Total yarn production amounts to 20 kg per household, per year, yielding a total income of Rs 154. A knitting household produces 20 sweaters per year, yielding earnings of Rs 124. As a result, the heavier spinning work is largely carried out by the lower income households. Returns to households at only Rs 0.30 to Rs 0.40 per hour are very low. An eight-hour day yields just over Rs 3 whereas the daily wage rate for unskilled labour is around Rs 10. The low economic value of part-time woollen textile production is limiting to women's status. Moreover, the potential link between a woman's income-earning capacity and her social power is dependent on the extent of her control over her earnings from her work. Existing cultural conventions severely limit such control.

On the face of things, the area looked highly suitable for such a project. However, even though the new device was mechanically very efficient—a 100 per cent increase in hourly productivity over the traditional charkha was achieved under field test conditions—impact was not all that could have been hoped for.

Despite the original plan to field test 50 improved spinning devices, only eight were eventually tested in a total of 10 households over a period of seven to eight months. By December 1982, only two of these were still being used by cottage spinners. A number of things seem to have gone wrong. First, the technology was much more complex than the spinners were used to. Constant machine repairs were necessary and this was a major factor in their rejection.

Second, the area chosen for field testing is dominated by non-Bhotia families, who work on a put-out system controlled by the Ghandhi Ashram. Since women in this area have too many other tasks to allow them to spend more than two or three hours a day spinning, investment in an improved device led to very little economic gain. It would have been impossible for such women to pay back loans for the device (Rs 650) from the proceeds of the two hours spinning a day they had time for. Finally, the difficulties encountered in changing to a complicated machine, requiring expensive maintenance were simply not worthwhile given the insignificant increase in income resulting from their use.

The new device, however, was found to benefit the sample of Bhotia households engaged in independent production. Here productivity increases were made both in yarn production and in weaving. As a result, Bhotias could raise overall production and incomes by over 60 per cent per annum. Thus, it looked as if the new device could bring significant benefit to such households.

There were three problems, however. The majority of Bhotias live in very remote areas which would make provision of repair facilities extremely difficult and therefore costly. Bhotia households prefer to spin hand-carded wool on the traditional charkha. Slubbing the wool eliminates the need for hand carding and plying, while the improved yarn quality reduces time lost in weaving due to breakages. But the process is carried out by slubbing institutions and the Bhotias have found these unreliable. Resistance to dependence on an institutional system would therefore negate, in practice, one of the benefits of the new device. Finally, raw materials are not available in unlimited supplies. Wool is, in fact, becoming scarcer for independent spinners in this area. Thus, if the new device was to be taken up by some of the wealthier, more centrally located Bhotia families, their increased productivity could result in an upsurge of open unemployment among less

Women in northern India help to support their families through wool-spinning.

resourceful Bhotia families. If the new device did catch on to any extent, raw materials would have to increase by 55 per cent to guarantee against open unemployment.

Although the improved machine was mechanically much more efficient than the existing spinning devices, it was rejected for a variety of socio-cultural, economic or locational reasons which should have been identified by a base line survey, prior to the introduction of the new device. Of particular interest is the fact that the non-Bhotia women simply did not have the time to take advantage of the more productive device. As so often happens, the macro-economic issues of the project were ignored: the device could well improve the incomes of some Bhotia spinners, but only at the expense of putting others out of work in the face of limited raw materials.

Spinning Muslin Yarn in India Muslin spinning is engaged in only by women. Characteristically, pre-spinning, as well as spinning, is done only by hand. Through the Khadi and village industry system, gins, and draw-frames to carry out pre-spinning operations, as well as a seven-spindle muslin charkha (spinning device) are distributed at subsidized rates to women spinners. Total cost of such a package is Rs 1,300 per spinner.

The women involved in this industry find the pre-spinning activities very tiring. They also require a lot of time—two days—for every six days spinning time. There is a good demand for muslin khadi, but attracting more women into the industry will depend largely on being able to increase productivity and returns to labour, through technological improvements in the ginning and drawing processes.

A rural development agency in South India has been attempting to solve this problem so that the women have more income to spend on improving the nutrition of their children. Equipment used elsewhere in the textile industry has been found unsuitable. Research is well under way on developing special devices. These will be manually operated as most of the spinners live in villages without electricity.

The question to ask here is whether the same mistakes will be made in developing and introducing improved technologies as with the new wool-spinning devices in Northern India. The

Muslin Spinning in South India

degree of involvement that the rural development agency has with the women spinners, suggests that any technological improvements developed and introduced under their control may stand a good chance of success.

Tie and Dye Co-operative in Tanzania Funds were made available by a development agency to a group of 30 women in rural Tanzania, members of the National Women's Party, who had organized themselves to produce inexpensive tie and dye clothing and household items. As part of this venture they had also developed management, accounting, marketing and purchasing skills. Research showed that there was a demand for the product in the area. Potentially, the project could supplement the incomes of the 30 women, as well as giving them the incentive to work co-operatively in small industry.

The project appears to have failed in just about every way possible. First, it was found that only the richer women in the village participated. Second, no management, marketing or purchasing skills were provided. Third, the group never worked as a co-operative—each member purchased raw materials and sold products individually, and no accounts or receipts were kept. Work eventually came to a stop because the caustic soda and dye, required for the process, were imported and a shortage of foreign exchange made it impossible to obtain them.

Dyeing in Mali and The Gambia A development agency organized a cloth-dyeing training programme in The Gambia at the request of the Malian Ministry of Rural Development. The programme sought to improve the technical skills of 12 representatives from eight community development centres which included cloth production as part of their activities. After returning from the Gambia, participants taught their newly acquired skills to roughly 100 members of the eight centres.

Production and sale of processed cloth was initially chosen as a viable activity for rural women, after a careful survey which had ruled out other likely projects, such as market gardening and poultry rearing. Its advantages were that there was a sizeable market for the product; it was a traditionally accepted activity for women, and (unlike market gardening) it was a year-round operation which could be integrated into the women's daily schedule.

Having inaugurated training and production units in rural centres, it quickly became apparent that not all the cloth produced could be sold in the immediate locality. There was, however, a flourishing market for tie-dye in Bamako. This was largely being met by cloth imported from other West African countries. It was thus decided to open a centre in Bamako to commercialize the cloth made in rural Mali. It was found, however, that designs and quality could not compete with imported cloth. There was a need to upgrade skills—hence the organization of the training course in The Gambia.

Just two months after the training programme, cloth using Gambian designs and colours was available in the Bamako store from two different participating groups. Most of this cloth had been produced by group members who had not been in Banjul but who had been taught by one of the participants. Most of this new cloth was immediately sold. Sales in the Bamako outlet doubled in the following year.

In the process of identifying an income-generating activity, dyeing was chosen because it could generate an even flow of income throughout the whole year. The way in which the skills were transferred between countries is worthy of note. People whose incomes depend on markets at home and abroad are not always willing to devote time and effort to providing training to potential competitors from nearby countries. The way in which women trained in The Gambia were then able to transfer their new skills to other women at home is also significant. There was also a substantial market to be met through import substitution.

Carpet Weaving in Iran As part of a government industry programme for the development of rural, non-farm employment opportunities, a survey of activities, needs and potentials was carried out in a poor district in Kurman. Off-farm job opportunities were very limited, but every family had sheep, which provided good quality wool. All women had primitive horizontal carpet looms, and they produced carpets of poor quality; older, finely woven carpets, with similar designs, were selling at a premium; fine quality wool from the sheep was being sold to city merchants leaving the weavers of Kurman itself without good raw material; dyeing facilities were not locally available. There were a few modern looms in the area, but they belonged to the merchants, who chose to employ men. These male carpet-makers were able to produce carpets of excellent quality, which provided them with good returns.

It was learned that large copper mines would be developed in the area in the next 10 years. They would certainly attract many men away from weaving and would also raise incomes in the area, thus expanding the market for carpets. Based on this knowledge, and the information from the feasibility study, it was decided that it would be worthwhile introducing a programme to upgrade the carpet-weaving skills of the women in the area. The idea was to help them form a co-operative through which wool could be processed locally. The co-operative would increase the members' production by giving them better quality raw materials; subsidizing the cost of new looms so that they could purchase their own equipment;

upgrading their skills so they would still be able to produce their own traditional patterns but in carpets of a much better quality; teaching the best of the weavers to read graph patterns so they would be able to introduce more colours and new designs.

Through local home economics agencies, the women were brought together and the project was discussed with them. It was discovered that the new vertical looms could not be introduced into their homes because the roofs were too low and there was not enough light inside. This problem was solved by suggesting that the subsidy to cover the cost of the loom should also include the cost of materials needed to build a very simple shed onto the home, where two looms could be put back to back. The beams, the supports and tin sheets for the roof would be given as a grant by the Government but the women, along with their families, would construct the shed, thus giving their labour as their contribution to the project.

A government subsidy covered half of the cost of the looms and the women paid the rest—10 per cent as initial deposit, with the remainder to be paid over the next year from women's earnings. This was feasible because earnings for a year were projected at three times the cost of the loom. The 10 per cent deposit (US$15) was a small amount for the women to raise from family sources. They did this with great enthusiasm, because ownership of the loom made them credit-worthy in the village economy.

The women were then given the raw materials from local co-operatives, along with instructions on design and quality. A master weaver assisted in the initial mounting of the warp on the new looms, started them off, and provided periodic supervision. The master weaver lived in the village and the women could go to him if they ran into difficulties. One master weaver supervised 15 looms with great ease. While the carpet weaving was in progress, the co-operative extended credit to the women to cover the items that women generally provide for their households, such as flour, salt, oil, tea, sugar and lentils.

After one carpet was finished, which took from three to seven months, the women could sell it, either to the co-operative, or to the trader—whichever paid a better price. The co-operative society calculated the basic weaving costs of the carpet and directly on completion of production, paid this base unit sum to the woman, after deducting any advance she had taken. The carpet was then evaluated by an expert and the woman paid 50 per cent of the difference between the estimated value and the basic unit cost. This acted as a good incentive to women to produce very fine carpets. Later on, private dealers decided that women were more reliable than men, kept their promises and worked regularly. Eventually, dealers began to induce women in nearby districts to take up fine quality weaving. This process was also helped by the fact that men were migrating to the towns in search of better job opportunities.

The project is thought to have worked because it was based on the careful assessment of prevailing socio-economic conditions, locally available skills and raw materials, and because there was a strong demand for the product. The opportunity to own their own looms, along with initial supervision and support provided in an appropriate manner, enabled the women to enter a commercial operation formerly accessible only to men. Eventually, they were able to be independent of any continuing government assistance.

Perhaps the most important point in this project was the way in which the co-operative enabled women—who needed cash daily, to provide basic goods for their families—to draw credit from co-operative funds during a production time which could last up to seven months. Many of the more productive returns on investment and labour often require a long waiting period: this is a useful example of how women can provide for their families while waiting for payment.

Spinning in Upper Volta Women's groups in the Dori region of Upper Volta identified the traditional practice of cotton spinning as a case for agency assistance in the development of income-generating projects. Originally, credit was provided to women in the form of cotton. The agency was to be reimbursed after the cotton was spun into thread and sold. Local cotton was not available, so processed cotton was purchased for which a comb was needed to separate the cotton. Many women were unwilling to pay the added expense of the comb and dropped out of the project. Follow-up for reimbursement posed difficulties, since market outlets had not been adequately studied to determine saleability and the women had difficulties in selling the thread. Problems also arose from the practice of distributing the cotton, which reinforced the 'something for nothing' mentality. Many of the women did not fully understand or accept the credit reimbursement conditions. As a result there were many hard feelings when the time came for repayments. Consequently there remained an underlying sentiment that the agency was acting as a police-person to ensure repayments rather than as a facilitator, trying to increase development opportunities.

Despite these setbacks, there were some positive aspects to the project. A strong basis for group formation developed, and the practice of collecting dues to form communal cash funds was established. A secondary project resulted from the cotton project, when women decided to utilize their communal fund to purchase sorrel seeds to make a fermented seed cake. This cake preserves well and is in high demand. The project proved very successful and was planned and implemented solely by the women, using their own resources.

Clearly, care needs to be taken to see that loans for ventures which have a low chance of economic return are not issued as this can put beneficiaries in a very difficult position. In this care, although the spinning project was a failure, the women were able to learn from their mistakes and apply this to choosing and participating in more profitable work.

Broadloom Weaving in Ghana In the Kumasi area of Ghana, the only major commercial activity, other than farming, is the weaving of Kente cloth (made from narrow strips of material) which is highly prized and can be sold at a very high price. The weaving is traditionally carried out on narrow handlooms, no more than 7 inches wide. It is a major occupation of men and boys in most villages: there is a taboo against women weaving as it is thought to cause infertility.

The staff of the technology centre located in Kumasi

believed that productivity could be greatly increased by using the broadloom instead of the narrow loom and, without wishing to replace the traditional craft, the staff thought that some weavers might like to learn to operate a broadloom. More importantly, they believed that the taboo for women might not apply in the case of the broadloom (different sitting/working position), so that weaving could at last provide a much needed source of income to rural women as well as men.

The project has had a checkered history. Over the years, several men and women have been trained to operate the broadloom. To a very limited extent, women have benefited from the new loom—one woman has set up her own weaving business and several others have been employed as weavers—but it was hoped that many more would have gone on to establish small businesses. Up-take has been limited, mainly because of the slender profit that can be made, given the high price of yarn (most cotton is imported). For the past year, there has been no yarn available in Ghana, and all weaving has come to a halt.

Spinning Silk in Bangladesh   Ericulture is a simplified form of sericulture and produces a silk somewhat less valuable than that woven from mulberry leaves. When looking for an appropriate income-earning activity for rural women in one area of Bangladesh, a development agency chose ericulture as the basis for some of its projects. The advantages of ericulture are many: the caterpillars feed on castor leaves which grow abundantly throughout village areas; the castor plant produces leaves every three months; the caterpillars are easy to care for and have a shorter life cycle than mulberry caterpillars, so that earning can commence within 45 days. The very young (14 years and up) can be taught to spin; and there are ready markets for spun yarn throughout the country.

Many women wanted to participate, but they needed training. They elected one of their number to spend two months at a training centre, where she was taught culture processing, de-gumming of cocoons and the operation of the spinning wheel. On her return to the village, she passed on her knowledge to the other co-operative members.

The development agency purchased a spinning wheel costing TK 250 (£8.00) for each of the members, which was to be paid back from their earnings. It was found that each spinner had her own peculiarities which led to modifications of the machines; good results were not obtained if women tried to

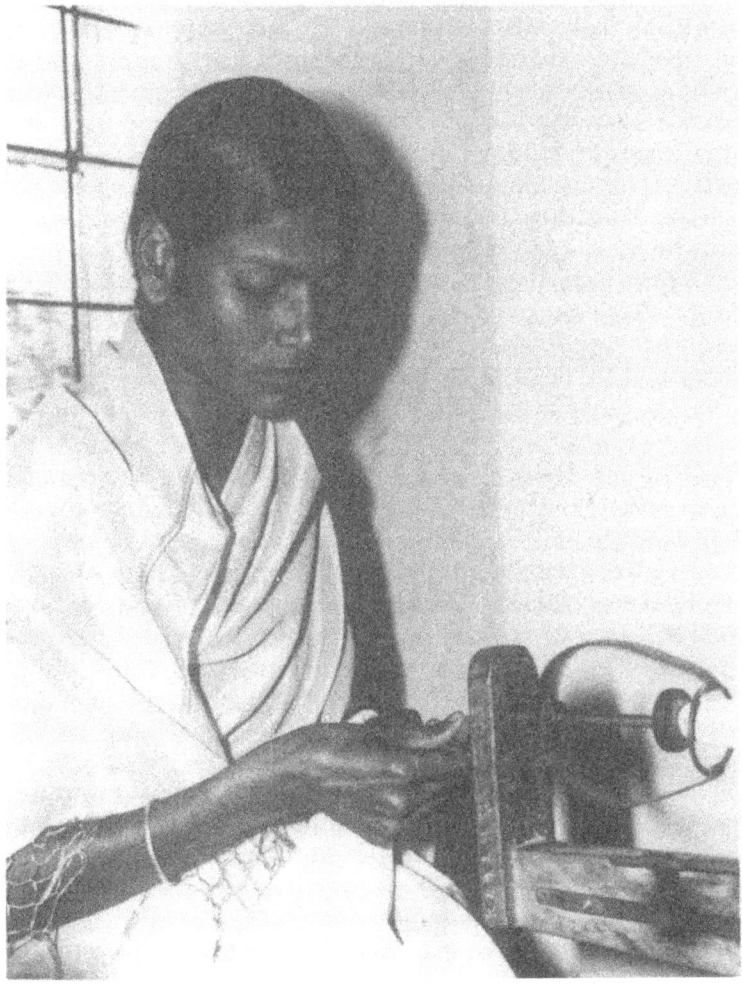

Increasing numbers of women in Bangladesh find employment in their own homes in silk production.

share the same machine. When a woman has produced sufficient yardage to sell, the trainer pays her, then re-sells in quantity to wholesalers. Within a few weeks, a novice is spinning 728 metres daily: an expert can spin 1,820 metres daily and earn TK 7-8 for a day's work.

A series of misfortunes resulted in the loss of the original stock of caterpillars and eggs. A voluntary agency then supplied a new batch which, in the second generation, proved to be diseased. Finally, the development agency purchased eggs from a breeding centre. Three ericulture huts of mud and thatch roofs have been constructed and strung with shallow baskets, each holding several hundred eggs from the overhead rafters. Thus they are inaccessible to rats and the women can guard against rat and ant infestation.

Despite some opposition to this development, especially from village conservatives who insist upon male dominance and the perpetuation of purdah, the operation has been successful. As women become income earners, they also gain prestige, both in the village and in the home.

Tailoring and Sewing Co-operatives in Tanzania   A development agency was asked for funds for a number of tailoring/sewing co-operatives. Each co-operative was to provide 15 to 20 jobs and was to produce school uniforms and clothing and household items demanded by the local community. None of these ventures appears to have had any great success.

A number of problems arose. In one case, the problem appears to have been that the choice of sewing machine type was made by men, who were far from the project site; electric sewing machines were chosen even though there was no electricity in the project village—a prime example of inappropriate technology, which occurs more often than it should! In another case, the sewing machines were stolen before the project even started. Another was discontinued, because of severe cash-flow problems, despite assistance with business management from a woman co-operative development officer and assistance with marketing from the Small Industries Development Organization (SIDO).

Textiles in Swaziland   The Women in Development Project in Swaziland sought to complement the low incomes derived from male migrant work, and to increase the production capacities of the local communities. As participating women did not consider training helpful, unless incomes were generated almost immediately, emphasis was placed on the initiation of local industries that could quickly produce cash incomes. While cash crop agriculture was examined as one option—since it would complement existing skills and activities—the decision was made to pursue craft-type activities, such as patchwork and weaving, which it was believed would provide more immediate returns.

Emphasis was placed on those products which would not require a great deal of training, could be produced manually, and had a ready market locally. After initial training, groups were organized as preco-operatives to be managed by the participating women. Eventually, it was planned that all work groups would be formed into one co-operative society, which would facilitate bulk purchasing of raw materials and collective marketing. After 12 months there were nine pre-co-operatives producing a variety of goods, ranging from socks for the Swazi police and school uniforms for local schools, to crochet work, sisal work and mohair spinning. When groups were initially formed, salaries were paid by the project out of its training budget. After a few months, however, salaries were completely covered by sales and borrowed funds for initial salaries were repaid. At this stage, 180 women were productively employed and a further 200 were awaiting either training, equipment, or the development of new product lines.

Incomes were found to vary according to product lines. The highest incomes came from knitting and sewing for the police and schools, which provided regular orders under contract. The lowest incomes came from crochet work and sisal weaving, for which there was little local demand. Average incomes were US$12.50 per month representing an increase of about 40 per cent on existing incomes.

Given that project-trained producers seem to have flooded the market with existing product lines, and given also that marketing difficulties seem to arise most with products geared to more distant markets, an attempt is now being made to identify more locally marketable products, such as bakery goods, soap, candles and paper. Emphasis is being placed on agriculture, and for this purpose an agricultural expert has been added to the staff to identify suitable projects and to give training and technical assistance. Potential projects include sericulture, beekeeping and pig raising.

This case study tends to reinforce the believe that, if the aim is to raise the incomes of rural women, handicrafts have a limited potential. After a few months of operation, the project had already found itself flooding the locally available market for crochet work, patchwork, and other handicrafts, and was looking for activities with a more established local market such as beekeeping (honey), soap and candles.

School Uniforms in Botswana   Bothakga Handknits was started in 1974 by a Botswanan woman with little formal education. Today it has 30 female employees and a turnover of 137,000 pula annually.

The proprietor has remarkable marketing skills and is constantly on the lookout for new areas into which to expand. As a result of preliminary surveys, she became aware of the fact that many schools were importing their uniforms and knitwear, thus failing to provide Botswana with job opportunities and also needlessly drawing on foreign exchange. Since knitwear and school uniforms were items produced by her firm, she set about the business of capturing the market for herself. The immediate problem seemed to be that most of the head teachers believed that anything made in Botswana could not be of as good a quality or value as something imported.

The proprietor sent out letters to schools inviting them to support local products. Accompanying the letters were samples of the most common items of school uniform. A letter of endorsement also went out to the schools from the Ministry of Commerce and Industry asking them to support local industries.

The response was an overwhelming one, with promises of future support coming in from those schools that had already placed orders with other suppliers. It was obvious that the firm could only meet this potential demand if additional machines were purchased and more workers trained. The promise of orders was used by the proprietor to secure a loan from the Government, through its rural small industry scheme.

Fishing Net Manufacture in India In Tamil Nadu, there is a great deal of hand net-making not only in the fishing villages, but also inland where it provides an important source of income in dry zones where there are several months of agricultural activity and no alternative employment. This work is done entirely by women. Recently, the government, has allowed the import of a large Japanese net-making machine triggering off concern about likely repercussions on rural employment.

For the moment, it appears that both hand-made nets and machine-made nets are still in demand. However, as is so often the case, the village women who make the nets are exploited by the merchants in Madras. They buy the nylon twine in bulk and take it to the women for making up into nets. They pay between Rs 12 and 15 per kilo of finished net. As it takes about one month to make up 1 kg of 1-inch mesh net, this works out at about 50 paise income a day. A local NGO has been involved in trying to get a better deal for these women. A project was developed with the Nirlon Company, who produce the nylon twine, whereby 20 girls organized by the NGO received nylon twine directly from the company and sold it back through the NGO at Rs 60 per kilo. In other words, by cutting out the middlemen, income from such work was quadrupled. The project ran successfully for three years, but stopped when the NGO moved to a different area. There are plans to repeat the project here, but the merchants (middlemen) are strongly established in this area and there is a great deal of resistance to plans for such a project.

Given the low productivity of such work (even when middlemen are not involved, daily wages are only Rs 2 per day), the NGO is also interested in the possibility of locating and introducing a small-scale machine for use by the women in making nets at the village level.

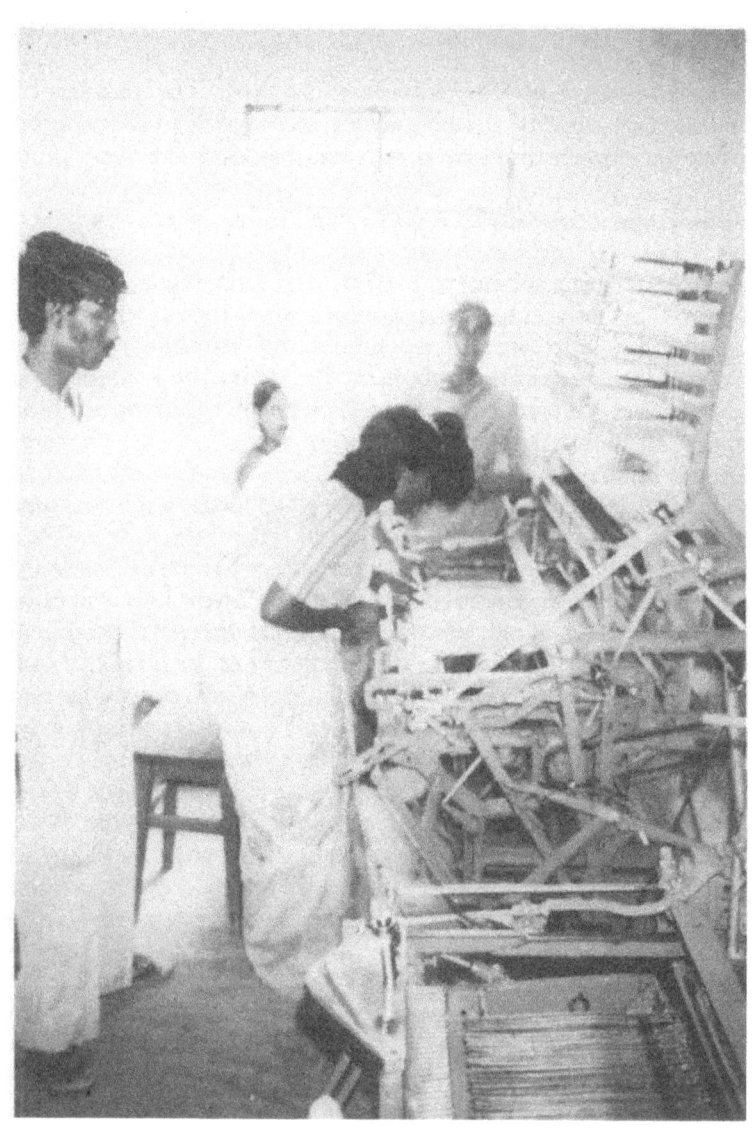
Machines such as this could enable village women to make fishing nets locally.

Rope Making in Sri Lanka   In Sri Lanka, coir is slowly attracting more attention, both from the Government, and from local and foreign private enterprise. New undertakings drawn to Sri Lanka through the establishment of the Free Trade Zone, tend to concentrate on the area where these commercial benefits apply. In the case of coir mat production this means that factories will be established far from the source of the raw material, and from where the labourers are accustomed to this work and depend on it for employment. Thus, although a policy of encouraging local processing of mats is better than exporting coir yarn to European carpeting firms, it will not necessarily benefit the thousands of women rope-makers of Sri Lanka's south coast.

A Dutch group, working with the Government's small industry department, has been running an income-generating project for women on the South Coast in an attempt to show that small-scale decentralized production, based in the area of raw material and skill availability, is more practicable than larger-scale production in Colombo. The project also aims to assist women directly who are interested in earning a higher income than they can with yarn making alone.

The project, which is a collective production unit for coir mat manufacture, encompasses all stages in the process—from retting through husking, spinning, rope-making, dyeing and mat-making. It has been running for five years and has a hundred women involved at different stages of the manufacturing process.

Since many women, rather than the local traders (who supply the export market) were now supplying the production unit with rope, resistance was obviously experienced. Threats were made to refuse to buy ropes in the future if the project collapsed, but the women felt more confident as a group than they would have done individually. One trader raised his price to try to attract supplies back, but the project counteracted by raising its price too. A potential problem is that the husk dealers, the suppliers of raw materials, who work closely with the rope dealers, may cut off the source of supply of husks to those women involved in the project.

Only 30 per cent of raw material on the island is currently

A stage in coir-processing, Sri Lanka.

being used in the coir business. There is thus a good basis for expansion if women coir workers can gain access to this material and can be provided with improved technology, credit and training, plus the confidence and support, to hold their own against the husk and rope traders and go into mat-making in their own right. Various government departments have, however, failed to give their support to women coir workers to form their own small-scale industries, even though dispersed small-scale industrialization is supposedly part of the Government's overall policy. Marketing problems still need to be looked into too. Although there is thought to be a good local market, which would be easier for women's groups to reach without institutional support, 75 per cent of the output of the current project is exported.

Summary As with the food processing industries, a common theme in this sector is the important role of appropriate technology. The experiences, to date, however, are far from satisfactory, and reveal very clearly that technology by itself is not enough.

A second theme in the textile-based industries is the importance of the put-out system—something not found in food processing because of hygiene problems. There is obviously a great need to find ways of enabling rural women to overcome exploitation by traders or middlemen, and develop small industries aimed at local markets which they can own and manage themselves.

The third factor is the shift in demand within the textile industry from low income goods, such as khadi, to high income goods, such as muslin and silk. This trend can be expected to speed up, as rural incomes increase with development. Project selection should take swings in demand into consideration and plan for women's involvement in the growth, rather than the declining industries.

Fourth, supplies of raw material—dyes, yarn, copra, wool—appear to be a common problem in these industries. Where possible, ways should be investigated of overcoming these by involving women in the production of such inputs for supply to other women's groups. The obvious limiting factor in this strategy will be access to land—more of a problem in some countries than in others.

Finally, more information is needed, through research, on women's involvement in the related footwear industry. This does not need to be leatherwork. In parts of West Africa, for example, women make shoes for their own children from old tyres—why not for sale? Similarly, in Bangladesh, women make footwear from jute attached to rubber-soled sandals.

3. BUILDING MATERIALS, HOUSING AND HOUSEHOLD GOODS

Apart from food and clothing, the other major category of basic goods, for which rural communities have a requirement is that of building materials for houses and storage structures (for crops and water); semi-durable household items such as stoves, furniture, mats, water filters, room dividers, brooms, pots and cooking/eating utensils; and a whole range of everyday consumables such as soap, salt, candles, matches and charcoal. Traditionally, such items (perhaps with the exception of candles and matches) have been made in the rural areas, using locally available materials, where their manufacture provides productive employment for a great many people.

Again, women have always played an important role in these industries. Many of Asia's lime burners are women, and traditional brick-making provides employment for rural women in many parts of the Third World. Women are traditionally responsible for roofing houses and other buildings in most countries of Eastern and Southern Africa; and, almost everywhere, women have had the responsibility for building structures/containers for storage purposes. In most cases they have also undertaken the manufacture of all things related to the kitchen such as stoves, pots and simple cooking/food utensils and equipment. Traditional soap-making is a female activity everywhere. In Africa, the traditional salt industry is totally in the hands of women and they are heavily involved in this activity in other parts of the world. Women are also involved in the making of charcoal and are totally responsible for this in parts of Africa and the South Pacific.

As with the food and clothing industries, these traditional industries are characterized by low-level technology and low returns to labour. Many, such as bricks, soap and salt, have gone into decline following the introduction of capital-intensive plants which have been established in the course of industrial development, and have flourished in an economic environment created to support maximization of output, rather than maximization of employment.

Others, such as lime burning, thatching and pottery, have gone into decline in the face of competition from new modern products such as portland cement, galvanized roofing sheets and whiteware china or aluminium pots which are frequently imported or, at best, manufactured in fairly capital-intensive plants in urban areas.

Encouragingly, a few attempts are being made to revive rural employment opportunities in these industries, either by upgrading traditional techniques (brick-making, lime-burning, salt manufacture), or by scaling down modern technology or through new technology developments, and introducing these to rural communities so that they can compete with modern products (small-scale cement plants, small-scale whiteware manufacture, fibre-reinforced roofing sheets). It is unfortunate that when such initiatives have been taken, they have often been aimed at men, sometimes to the total exclusion of women, who are traditionally responsible for such activities.

The case studies in this section look at projects which have been specifically aimed at assisting women, rather than men, to establish viable rural industries and create female employment opportunities in the building and household durables/consumables industries. Some, such as sisal-cement roofing sheets in Kenya, involve the introduction of a new product as well as new skills. Others, such as stove-making in Indonesia and Senegal, look at attempts to increase women's incomes by producing new products using existing skills. Some, soap-making in Tanzania and Mali, are concerned with the employment of women in scaled-down modern technologies to produce high quality modern products. Others, such as caustic potash in Ghana, represent an attempt to create a rural industry by increasing the productivity of an existing labour-intensive activity.

Sisal-Cement Roofing Sheets in Kenya Taita district is in the south-east corner of Kenya. It has the distinction of being the only area in Kenya known to have an operating sisal-cement production unit. It is particularly interesting because the unit is in a rural area and, moreover, is run by a women's group.

It was the interest of a woman community development worker in the potential of sisal-cement as an income-generating activity, which brought the UK originators of the technique to the area. During a visit in 1979, they felt that the proposal to establish a project with a women's group was interesting, but not as a full-time commercial venture. Funds were obtained from an appropriate technology agency in the USA and given as a grant to the women's group to initiate a production unit.

As a first step, the community development worker and the manager (male) of the local craft training centre attended a training course in Nairobi along with others, from all over Kenya, who were interested in starting projects. On their return, they taught the techniques to the women. A shed for the new unit was built and partly roofed with sisal-cement sheets. Understandably, this first batch of sheets were of low quality.

Once the unit was established, the women met once a week to make sheets, and boys and girls also participated. Productivity is extremely low—20 women make only four sheets a day—but this is because the project is seen partly as a social occasion and also because there is no division of labour, with everybody particpating in all the activities. In practice, only four to six of the women are actually making the sheets. Between 200 and 300 sheets had been made up to February 1982. Some had been sold for houses, others for animal sheds. Thirty had been used for a chicken shed. There was a feeling that the sheets were unsafe and, therefore, only suitable for these sheds. Some sheets were stolen, emphasizing the need for a secure store.

In the spring of 1982, there were 60 sheets in stock, and orders for 60 more. However, the stock sheets had been incorrectly stacked and many of them were cracked as a result.

Cement prices rose from 35 shillings per 10 kg in 1979 to 68 shillings in 1982. However, the sale price of the roofing sheets has taken account of this. A 1.5 m sheet costs 24.20 shillings to manufacture, if no allowance is made for labour, and sells for 30 shillings. An equivalent galvanized iron roofing sheet sells for 50 shillings. The women could easily raise the selling price of their sheets to allow for a more realistic return for their labour.

The women were found to be measuring cement and sand with 1 kg cooking fat tins. The proportions were 12 tins of cement to 16 tins of sand. They did not realize that the volume of one tin would not automatically give 1 kg of cement or sand, due to the different density of fat. The thickness of each sheet varied according to how much care was taken by each of the six women in their work.

Since September 1980 there has been no interest shown in the project by the Ministry of Community Development and, with the originator of the project no longer there, the craft training centre (CTC) manager has been solely responsible for finances, project development, and other management functions. He feels that the group is amateurish and would like CTC to

Pressing sisal-cement mortar into the roofing-sheet mould, in Kenya.

manage the project, with the women as joint shareholders. The women do not want this, but their position is weakened by a lack of support from the Ministry of Community Development and poor book-keeping skills. A solution is needed as the unit has now run out of cement and the women seem to be having difficulty in gaining access to more funds to purchase further raw materials.

The quality of production clearly needs to be improved and the treasurer, a member of the women's group, given training in book-keeping techniques.

This case study represents one of the few examples of an attempt to introduce new roofing technology to women in a part of the world where roofing is traditionally their responsibility. By and large, it is men who have been trained, rather than women! Apart from this, it should be noted that the type, nature and length of training given to the women was clearly insufficient to allow them to master a new technique, such as this completely. More intensive training, actually in the village, and frequent monitoring visits by instructors, and refresher courses by participants, are clearly needed until procedures become well established. Further technical training without financial and managerial training and backing is clearly insufficient. Advice on pricing and marketing of a new product is clearly needed; especially so, given the assumptions used when estimating the viability of units producing roof sheets, which included full-time work and year-round operation—in a situation where the need is for part-time work and where demand for the product is seasonal. It is also evident from this case that if production units become too reliant on external support, they are in danger of declining if such support is withdrawn. Finally, the attitude of the manager of the local craft centre, the only other person to have attended the training course in Nairobi, is of interest because it is so typical. It is obviously easier to blame the difficulties experienced in a project on the lack of skills of the participants, than to actively seek support to provide them with such skills.

Stove Factories in Indonesia   One of the major promoters of improved stoves in Indonesia has decided that the making of mud stoves and the time and effort-intensive method of training stove builders—who are then supposed to train others—is not a viable strategy. Attention has turned, instead, to the 'mass production' of ceramic liners, which allows the difficult work to be done centrally under supervision. This leaves only the unskilled work of coating the liner with mud to be carried out by individual households.

The first step has been to set up stove factories, on a pilot basis, to make the ceramic liners for trial and demonstration. Four thousand such liners are to be purchased by the Government through a World Bank forestry project, and installed free of charge in village houses. It is anticipated that the use of this number of stoves will demonstrate their efficiency in terms of wood savings, and stimulate demand for the liners, which cost about 590 rupiyahs.

To meet this initial demand for liners, the NGO involved in stoves promotion visited many pottery villages in the rural areas in Central Java, to investigate possibilities of establishing production units based on existing skills. Since the traditional products of these pottery villages are not in much demand any more, there was obviously enthusiasm about the idea of diversifying into a new product. Two villages with highly skilled workers were selected and factories established.

It is the women who traditionally do the pottery work in the village. However, they have not been trained to make the ceramic liners. Instead, they are expected to continue making their traditional pots, which the men then form into liners. There are three male employees to every one female employee in each factory. Men are also in the supervisory jobs, earning 44,000 rupiyahs per month as opposed to 31,000 rupiyahs per month for the women and other men employees. This compares with an average wage in the area of 22,000 rupiyahs to 29,500 rupiyahs per month.

If stove liners become popular, there will be an enormous demand for these throughout Java, thus offering great potential for the creation of rural jobs. Women will clearly benefit from this, as the making of pots is something which is very obviously seen as a woman's job. They will not benefit as much as they might have done, however, if they had been given

Part of the process for village-level manufacture of ceramic stoves.

the training necessary to retain control of what is essentially a woman's industry.

There seems to be no reason why women could not be more fully involved in projects of this type and given training so that they can have access to at least *some* of the more highly paid jobs. However, if the women, who are the intended users and beneficiaries of improved stoves, do not necessarily have access to cash of their own, will there, in fact, be an effective demand for mass produced stoves?

Stove Builders in the Sahel In the Sahel countries, the effects of rapid deforestation, due to drought, overgrazing and the expansion of agriculture, have been well documented. Following various reports, stove programmes have been initiated in all countries in the Sahel region as a partial solution. The Senegalese programme was initiated in 1980 with the aim of decreasing the amount of wood used in cooking. It has also indirectly created jobs in stove-building for rural women and men.

Two different stove models were developed. A basic single

pot-hole, mud, chimneyless stove was designed by potters from the Louga district. It is claimed that this stove is 30 per cent more efficient than the open fire. Spurred on by the enthusiasm of one of the potters, the women were trained to build their own stoves. Much of the pottery in the Louga district is produced by women and it is believed that the wide diffusion of stoves here could be attributed to the skills of the women and their percipience in anticipating of a fuelwood crisis.

In other areas, it appeared that some people wanted a two-pot chimney stove. The programme adopted a model developed in Upper Volta. Two teams, consisting of builders, promoters, and monitorices were trained by a development agency to distribute these stoves for field testing.

The promoter visits the village where the first task is to create awareness and generate enthusiasm for the stoves. The masons then train interested men and women to build the new stove. The best results found to occur after women-only training sessions.

The development worker then returns to instruct the new owners on the proper use and maintenance of the stove. After this training it is expected that villagers will maintain and rebuild their own stoves. The development agency has also established a team based in Dakar that has been training mainly unskilled and unemployed women and men to establish small stove construction businesses in their villages. In some villages women have formed associations to raise sufficient funds to pay these masons for their work.

Approximately 5,000 stoves have been built, of which 2,300 were Louga stoves. Eighty-nine per cent of the Louga stoves have been built by women, compared with 43 per cent of the chimney stoves. This implies that either the women prefer the chimneyless stove, or find it easier to build, or that men do not consider chimneyless stoves to have sufficient prestige, and so prefer not to build them. According to an evaluation, 65 per cent of a sample of 985 stoves were in daily use, the majority of these (77 per cent) being Louga stoves.

Soap-making Co-operative in Tanzania   In 1976, a group of 40 women in rural Tanzania formed themselves into a co-operative to make soap—a scarce article in the country and one which was thus in great demand. Assistance and encouragement was given by the local branch of the National Women's Organization which saw the need to develop a small-scale co-operative to provide employment for women. The project was also given the full support of SIDO and co-operative development officers in the district. Equipment was purchased with the help of a grant from Canadian University Service Overseas (CUSO).

When the business is operating at capacity, the 40 women work four days each per week—some in manufacturing, some in marketing. They work in three rented rooms of a private dwelling; conditions are far from ideal, and the lack of space seriously reduces their production. Although the demand for soap is great, the demand for coconut oil—the main ingredient in soap—is even greater. Supply of oil is scarce and irregular and, consequently, the prices are exhorbitant. Whenever the co-operative can secure oil, it immediately starts production. As the supply of coconut oil is so irregular, production is slow. However, whatever can be produced is easily sold.

This study demonstrates the danger of building an income-generating project on the basis of shortage of demand for a product, without fully investigating the availability of supplies of raw materials. Import bans frequently create opportunities for small local industries producing both consumer and producer goods. Often, however, some skilful technological assistance is required to take advantage of such opportunities —so as, for example, to get round the coconut oil problem by finding locally available alternatives. The co-operative in this case study had no such support.

Soap Making in Mali   In Mali, as in much of West Africa, women collaborate with their husbands to support the family. One group of women in the town of Markala, finding themselves unable to earn enough to feed and clothe their children adequately, decided to form a co-operative in an attempt to increase their incomes.

During the first year of the co-operative's life, members spent a considerable time discussing various income-producing possibilities. Deciding to upgrade and improve their existing skills, they began by organizing the collective gathering and sale of firewood, cloth dyeing, and the processing and selling of fish oil. Because cloth dyeing suited the women's schedules and interests, it became the principal revenue base for the co-operative. However, profit margins were low due to the high cost of raw materials for chemical dyeing and the labour intensiveness required by traditional indigo and mud techniques. So, hoping to expand their range of income-producing activities, the women began to experiment with different techniques of soap-making.

Mali's soap factory, Sepom, could not meet the local demand for laundry soap, and imported soaps were too expensive for most of the rural population. Thus, Malian women relied heavily on soap made locally, using traditional techniques to combine potash and local oils. These methods produced a soft soap which dissolved quickly and was often too caustic for consumer use. There was, therefore, considerable demand for good quality laundry soap at reasonable prices.

As the first step toward improving local soap production, the co-operative members found an expert from the Bozo ethnic group willing to show them how to make soap using caustic soda. In what is known as cold process soap-making, oil is melted and then allowed to cool to body temperature. At the same time a caustic soda solution is prepared and cooled. This solution is then added slowly to the oil, and the mixture stirred constantly until saponification occurs. The soap is then poured into moulds, allowed to harden, and is cut into bars for sale.

Co-operative members experimented with both fish and shea butter, the two oils most readily available. They found that fish oil produced a delicate soap which lathered extremely well. Because of the properties of this oil, however, long hours of stirring were required before saponification occurred, and a hard soap never resulted. Shea butter, on the other hand, produced a hard soap quickly, after only half an hour of stirring. Shea butter soap, however, did not lather well. Additionally, both soaps had an unpleasant odour which co-operative members were unable to mask with perfumes or local lemon grass. A final disadvantage was the high cost of imported caustic soda. Because of these constraints, the co-operative members only made a profit using cold-process techniques during periods of acute soap shortage and/or plentiful oil supply.

The fortunes of the co-operative changed with the timely visit in 1979 of a staff member of the Technology Consultancy Centre (TCC) in Ghana, who proposed that women should try the boiling or hot-process method of soap-making, a technique previously unknown to them. The boiling process offers several advantages. First, production costs are lowered as the proportion of caustic soda to oil is considerably less than in cold-process soap-making. Second, more soap is produced for a given quantity of oil, as water and fillers increase its bulk. Finally, the boiling process removes the strong odours of fish oil and shea butter.

Together, the co-operative members and their visitor experimented with boiling-process soap-making trying different combinations of shea butter (made from the shea nut), fish and peanut oils. They also calculated the production costs of soap based on the highest seasonal oil price and, having concluded that soap-making could indeed be a profitable venture, the co-operative's soap-making committee asked for TCC assistance in installing a soap-works based on the boiling-process method.

The first step was the installation of the soap-boiling tanks in the co-operative's courtyard. A local mason was hired for several days' skilled work while the women themselves carried the bricks, rocks and cement needed for installation. First, the tanks on their iron stands were put in place and mud bricks packed around three sides of the stands, creating a reinforced mud oven under the boiling tanks. A cement wall was then built around the tanks, filled in with rocks and finished with a thin layer of cement to create a platform on which the soap-makers could stand during the boiling process. The total cost of the soap-work's installation was 505,380 Malian francs (c.£500). A tin canopy to shelter the soap-makers from the rain was added later at additional cost. With the soap-works installed, the co-operative members produced four batches of boiling process soap of 150 litres each, under TCC supervision.

After a week of soap-making trials in the new works, the co-operative members were satisfied that they had acquired the basic techniques, and TCC's training role was complete. Over the months that followed, the Markala soap-makers continued to experiment with combinations of oils, fire intensity, timing of water addition and different fillers. They found a source of kaolin nearby and tried different methods of producing a kaolin powder fine enough to ensure increased soap hardness, smoothness, binding and transparency. The final product is a laundry soap which compares extremely favourably in quality and appearance with any industrially produced soap sold in Mali. The Markala co-operative product is a soap of which the members are justifiably proud.

The original group of three soap-makers has expanded to 10 women who have mastered all the production techniques. They, in turn, call upon about 10 others for labour on production days twice a week. Co-operative members who participate in soap-making are paid for their labour. All income from soap-making is held in a separate account, which was

The Markala soap co-operative in Mali.

initially used for the purchase of raw materials. Recently, however, on the basis of the soap-works' profits, the Markala co-operative had raised the monthly stipend received by each member by 25 per cent.

Though the technical aspects of soap production have been mastered, and local demand for high quality laundry soap met, a number of obstacles remain before the Markala soap-works can attain the co-operative members' goals. The co-operative's objective of production and sale of 2,000 bars of soap per week required that retail agents be set up in other Malian towns, as Markala itself cannot absorb so much. This has strained the co-operative's book-keeping system as the two literate members must keep up the written records of all co-operative undertakings, which now include management of a millet-grinding mill, as well as cloth dyeing and soap-making. Recently, an improved book-keeping and stock control system for the soap-works was established, though further training in book-keeping is still needed. In August 1979, the co-operative began bulk purchase of raw materials to increase profits by reducing production costs. Bulk purchasing, however, requires a re-evaluation of the working capital necessary for the soap-works, as well as an accurate stock control system and effective transport and storage facilities. These questions are currently being studied by co-operative members who may seek credit for expansion as well as technical assistance for co-operative accounting.

Other women's co-operatives in Mali have shown considerable interest in learning improved soap-making techniques. In January 1980 the Markala co-operative trained 15 representatives from nine rural women's groups in cold-process soap-making. The Markala co-operative has thus begun to act as a centre for diffusion of soap-making technologies to other women in Mali. These groups have begun local production and, depending on local oil supplies and group cohesion, it is likely that some will install boiling tanks in the future. It is hoped then that the transfer of soap-making technologies will strengthen other women's institutions in the country.

Co-operative members chose soap-making themselves on the basis of their own skills and interests, and local demand and resources; they were also very much involved in adapting the technology to their own needs and circumstances. Further, co-operative members controlled the nature and pace of new technologies introduced and made use of regional technological capacities to serve their own needs. The women in the co-operative were also willing to share their new skills with other women throughout the country and to participate actively in training others. This concern of rural women for the equal sharing out of opportunities to earn income is quite strong in many parts of Africa. In most villages, for example, women are traditionally content to work part-time in the interests of widespread employment: engaging in full-time activity would mean more income for some at the expense of no income for others.

Caustic Potash Making in Ghana The shortage of soap in Ghana has meant that many rural women's groups have a keen interest in making soap as an income-generating venture. However, there has been great difficulty in acquiring the caustic soda necessary for processing the pale, or bar soap, which is preferred by most consumers. As a result, in addition to encouraging the production of pale soap, the National Council of Women and Development (NCWD) has organized some projects for the production of caustic potash.

In one project, with the help of the Cocoa Research Station at Tafo and the Kuamoso State Palm Plantations, the women were taught how to burn dry cocoa pods and palm wastes in order to produce potash. Until then these were simply discarded. In another, the women were introduced to a kiln which was specially constructed by the engineering department of the university at the request of the NCWD. It was designed to simplify and speed the process of rendering down palm branches and banana peels into powder by burning. These women prepare large quantities of this powder and package it for selling on to others in the area who make the soap up into bars. There is a strong demand for the powdered caustic potash, because it is a product women are familiar with. Moreover, it considerably shortens the time the women previously spent in soap production and also saves them the firewood they would have to fetch or buy for day-long burning of the palm bunches and plantain peels.

There is another problem for soap-makers, however. Palm oil, one of the main ingredients of soap, is also in short supply. The main technology centre in the country is experimenting with substitutes such as cocoa butter, castor oil, neem oil, monkey cola (groundnut oil) shea butter and sunflower oil. The NCWD is collaborating with women's groups in carrying out field tests. Once a suitable oil extractor has been identified, it hopes to set up a women's group in the commercial production of sunflower and castor seeds, along with the extraction and sale of the oil to soap-makers.

Noteworthy in this study is the way in which the women are being helped to establish enterprises to make a product (caustic soda) which is needed by other women's businesses (soap-makers), or by rural women wanting to make soap at home, without the time and expense of making their own inputs. In addition, the attempt to identify alternatives to scarce palm oil, and develop appropriate technologies to process different types of oils, is an excellent example of how local technological expertise can be put to work for rural women.

Summary There are a number of common themes emerging from these case studies which need emphasis.

First, when women are given the necessary training and access to technologies, they take to modern versions of their own industries like fish to water. The fact that women make more appropriate producers of household-related equipment is very clearly illustrated by the African stove-making experience.

Second, the majority of case studies relate to clay-based and agro-based products, such as stoves, soap and caustic soda. There is a noticeable lack of activity in the wood- metal-based activities such as furniture-making.

Third, there is a paucity of case study material on women's involvement in a variety of other basic goods industries. In some cases, there are leads which can be followed up. For example, we know that attempts are being made in several countries—The Gambia, Indonesia and Nigeria—to increase productivity in the traditional salt industry through the introduction of solar equipment and other improved technologies. We also know of women's involvement in village level matchmaking in India and the attempts in various countries, such as Botswana and India, to introduce candle moulds to women's groups, as a basis for employment. There are scraps of information about women making brooms in Guyana and other countries of the Caribbean. Women in various West African countries have been taught how to make household-level water filters and cement water jars, but little is known about their experience in finding employment in such work after training. There is also some information on charcoal making in the South Pacific, using improved technologies, and others in Asia making fuel from compressed agro-wastes, such as rice husk. Similarly, simple machines have been developed in India which increase the productivity of tribal women involved in the production of leaf plates—a simple mould process under pressure which replaces laborious hand-stitching.

The potential for the involvement of rural women in the village-level production of all these items seems to be enormous. However, information on the extent to which they are already involved, or data on projects which have aimed to increase their involvement is not sufficient to gain a clear idea of what yet needs to be done. Experiences from the few case studies which are available in this category do, however, suggest that it is a promising area to pursue.

4. OTHER CONSUMER GOODS

Having taken care of the major basic consumer goods in rural communities, there are still a number of other items which are found in, or needed by most villages and which are, or could be, manufactured in the locality. Items, for example, normally required by rural institutions, such as day-care centres, schools and health clinics—toys, chalk, paper, blackboards, chairs, desks, pencils, baby scales, solar stills, cooling devices, bandages, bush ambulances, hospital beds. This also includes goods which are required by families in particular circumstances, such as illness (household medicines) or where there is some disability or defect (wheelchairs, low-cost health aids, low-cost spectacles). Goods which are nice to have, if they can be afforded, but which can be done without if necessary (torches, umbrellas, sanitary towels), also fall in this category.

There are two interesting characteristics about the demand for goods in this category. First, much of it is institutional (government, missions, rural development agencies), so that contracts can be placed with producers who have certain characteristics with which the institution is in some way concerned (e.g. co-operatives of the landless, women, youth, handicapped). Second, demand can be expected to increase considerably over time, as health and educational facilities in rural areas expand and improve, and as incomes in rural communities increase in real terms.

Many of the commodities involved are imported or produced in urban areas and then shipped out to rural areas. Apart from the expense of distribution, opportunities for productive employment in rural areas are also denied. Some Governments (e.g. India and Botswana) have used the opportunity to place contracts for school furniture, or other equipment, with particular types of small, rural producers, in much the same way as contracts are placed for school uniforms or police uniforms. Private institutions also sometimes use this method of giving work to poor families in their locality. The examples are all too rare, however, and those which do exist often involve no women in production.

Goods production, which is aimed at individual households, seems to fall into two categories. First, there are those which have been produced traditionally in rural areas (e.g. medicines) and which are losing markets to mass-produced modern goods (modern drugs). Second, there are those for which no suitable technology exists, as yet, to permit village-level production (e.g. sanitary towels, torches, umbrellas). Needless to say, many projects are underway, aimed at rectifying such problems, some of which do, or shall, assist rural women.

Not surprisingly, it was virtually impossible to find specific case study material on the experiences of women's employment in production of goods in this category. Of the three case studies included, two relate to the production of furniture and other equipment for government and private institutions in rural areas—day-care centre furniture and equipment in Jamaica; hospital beds in Bangladesh. The other relates to an attempt to protect and expand women's employment in the collection and manufacture of traditional medicines in India.

Day-Care Centre Equipment in Jamaica When planning its training for employment programmes, the Jamaica Women's Bureau sought advice from the Small Industries Division of the Industrial Development Corporation which estimated that, given the Government's increased interest in child-care, there would be an increasing demand for furniture and equipment for day-care centres. The basic skills required were carpentry and welding.

For the first training course, 48 out of 70 applicants were chosen. All these people were currently registered with the government's Special Employment Programme (SEP), which aimed at providing manual work for the very poor. Preference was given to those in the peak earning years, and to those who were the source of support for their families. Among the 48, were two men—two more than the number of women in any previous welding or carpentry course. Training lasted for eight months and included business and co-operative skills. The Government's Special Employment Programme (SEP) paid maintenance stipends during this period.

As the training period neared an end, it became clear that the newly trained welders and carpenters could not just open up a business the day training was completed. An apprenticeship period was needed to enable the women to begin production and to develop a co-operative structure. Continued support from the Women's Bureau and relevant government departments during this period was crucial. The group could not of course immediately generate enough income to cover its costs and the financial needs of its members, nor did the bureau have sufficient financial resources to fund this stage. Fortunately, the SEP agreed to continue member's stipends during the start-up phase. In addition, the bureau procured working capital grants from Canadian International Development Agency (CIDA) and Christian Action for Development in the Caribbean (CADEC) which were used to provide basic equipment and raw materials. The bureau found a rent-free government building to house the group.

Thus, the United Women's Welding and Woodworking Project began actual operation. Technically, the group remains in the preco-operative stage. To register as an official co-operative, they must be prepared to stop receiving the SEP payments: so far they are not economically strong enough to do this. The road from training to self-sufficiency has been a lot tougher than anticipated.

Shortly after the project commenced regular operation, the Women's Bureau reduced its level of support as staff time was needed to start new projects elsewhere. It was assumed that the group could cope by itself after receiving technical training and courses in co-operative management. This proved unrealistic; the women did not have a sound understanding of co-operative principles, the management structure was untried and not fully developed, not enough orders were generated in the first months to keep up production; and there was no proper book-keeping system.

A major problem arose out of the initial decision to manufacture day-care furniture and equipment. Demand was not nearly as high as anticipated and the project found it difficult to compete with the mass-produced goods imported from developed countries. The cost of raw materials began to increase and the furniture designs, while attractive, took considerable time to make. It thus became more difficult to make a profit. The women decided to expand the items manufactured to include desks, chairs, coffee tables, iron grilles for windows, household fixtures, ash trays and lamps, which they thought would be in demand locally. Currently most orders come from government ministries. A wider market is needed, but the women received no marketing training during their course and now need advice on this. Since many of these women already have some experience as small traders, an attempt is now being made to build on these skills with assistance from CADEC and other relevant agencies.

Of the original 48 participants, 26 women and one man remain. Some of those who dropped out were either unwilling or unable to shoulder the burdens and risks of running a co-operative enterprise. In other cases, participants left to take higher-paying jobs—testament to the success of the training effort. The remaining group are well aware of their problems and are intent on taking the steps necessary to put their enterprise on a solid footing. The co-operative's income currently averages US$1,000 to US$3,000 per month which is used for materials, utilities and operating costs. Rent is still subsidized by the Government as are salaries: grants from other agencies are used to support further training efforts and to bring in outside expertise.

Although there are still problems with this project, in many ways it has proved to be very useful. It has demonstrated that training in non-traditional skills is not only possible but beneficial, and can turn marginally employable women into skilled workers. It has generated considerable interest and news coverage and attracts visitors from all over Jamaica and from abroad. Most importantly, since the project began, more

Women welders in Jamaica.

women enrol in the regular skills training programmes run by the Government every year. Another important issue is that it shows how a small agency with limited resources can accomplish a great deal, simply by acting as a catalyst and drawing on the skills and resources of other agencies—both government and private.

The main point of interest in this case study is the way in which women were trained in non-traditional skills because these were the ones which market research indicated were necessary to gain productive employment. Any sex-stereotyping seems to have been overcome remarkably quickly—even to the extent of some trainees getting paid work outside the co-operative. The demonstration value of this project is tremendous. Another important point is the way in which the Women's Bureau executed the project with few resources of its own by drawing on existing resources (mainly government departments) elsewhere in the country and making these work for women.

Hospital Equipment in Bangladesh Gonoshasthaya Kendra is a private, indigenous agency which was organized in the aftermath of independence in Bangladesh to provide health services to a complex of villages around Savar about 20 miles north of Dhaka. It has a modern hospital and clinic at Savar, four sub-centres in nearby villages, with facilities for minor surgery and two beds for emergency patients. The clinic with its sub-centres covers all but the most urbanized part of the thana (district).

Part of the agency's work includes employment-oriented training and income-generating activities for landless women. The metal workshop has 22 workers or trainees, 17 of them are women or young girls. They manufacture hospital equipment, including beds and stationary bikes for physical therapy. The woodworking programme involves a few local women and about six girls as well as men. Because opportunities for women are few, their drop-out rate is well below that of male workers.

This is another useful example of women being trained in work which is generally done by men. In this case, however, the women are dependent for employment on the institution which trained them, as traditional prejudices remain firm in the area.

Traditional Medicines in South India Throughout India, the knowledge of when, how and where to gather and harvest plants and leaves with medicinal properties is retained by the tribal villagers. With a thriving demand for these herbs, middlemen have tended to move in to exploit the villagers—paying very low prices for raw materials. It was for this reason that a large rural development agency in the south became involved. The idea was to guarantee the villagers a stable demand for medicinal herbs at fair prices and at the same time to establish a rural processing unit to provide jobs for poor families (mainly women). Normally, middlemen removed the raw materials for processing by capital-intensive technology in the towns.

The unit employs about 25 people, most of whom are women. They are paid Rs 5 to Rs 8 per day. This is a good wage in this area—the maximum wage for casual farm work being Rs 5 per day. There is also an incentive system. There are two medical practitioners employed who are very knowledgeable about medicine production. The machinery used is not made on the premises, but has been adapted to specific needs. It is mainly manually operated, although there is a semi-automatic pill-making machine. The major processes are grinding and mixing; steam extraction; settling and pill-making. The pills and mixtures are labelled, boxed and sold through KVIC stores and chemists. None of the processes requires a high degree of skill.

There are about 120 branded products. The agency has numerous formulae for a range of products to treat all types of symptoms. Most of the mixtures are traditional; others have been revised and improved by the medical practitioners employed in the factory. Any profits are channelled back into the rural development agency to help pay for its non-commercial activities. Profit margins, however, are not very high because the factory pays good prices to the Tribals for raw materials and good salaries to its employees.

The success of the project lies mainly in its being able to tap a new market. The preparations it sells cost between Rs 2 and Rs 15 a package. Mass-produced city medicines cost twice as much for the same amount, which is out of the reach of most rural people. Guaranteed distribution and outlets through KVIC stores throughout the rural areas is also a benefit.

Although demand would permit an expansion of production, supply of raw materials is a constraint on this. There is no system or agent to ensure regular collections from the villages and there are seasonal constraints on the harvesting. The agency has started to grow limited quantities of its own herbs to try to even out the worst of the seasonal variations and give a more regular pattern to production.

Summary The obvious point to highlight in this section is the disappointing lack of case study material available and the somewhat experimental nature of that which could be found.

Women can obviously engage in the production of metal and wood products if they are given the necessary training and a chance to put the training into practice. Until problems of sex stereotyping are overcome in the private, commercial sector, the system of giving government contracts to women's co-operatives, or reserving certain markets for women's enterprises (as is done with small-scale industries in many countries) seems to be a necessary, if not sufficient, condition for helping women to share in the benefits of the growth in the 'other consumer goods' sector by supplying a part of the increase in demand.

Although there are, for the moment, no further detailed studies of projects, there are several leads which are encouraging and need to be followed through. Women are known to be involved in the manufacture of baby scales using local materials (rope, wood) in South India; they also find employment in the manufacture of chalks for schools. This latter form of employment is a KVIC industry: women can obtain credit for a chalk mould of gun-metal which costs about Rs 400. They mix a slurry of 70 per cent plaster of paris and 30 per cent slaked lime—this is a low-grade mixture developed especially by KVIC—and pour it into moulds before sun drying and packing. Return on investment is about 30 per cent. There is

Grinding ingredients for traditional medicines, South India.

no reason why women cannot make solar stills: women elsewhere successfully make solar dryers (Bangladesh, Guyana) and solar wax extractors (Kenya). Much research work is being done on adapting technologies to allow for the village-level production of wheelchairs, bush ambulances and low-cost spectacles (e.g. pedal-driven lens grinders). Once these are introduced, there is no reason why women, as well as men should not be involved in their production.

In Bangladesh, one private agency which deals mainly with job creation for rural women is well advanced with its plans to establish village units to produce pencils. These will substitute for imports from China. Another agency which also concentrates on employment for landless women in Bangladesh is working towards the establishment of village-level production of umbrellas. Agencies everywhere are interested in the concept of rural women's groups producing sanitary towels. However, even if cotton is grown locally, the process of bleaching cotton wool to make it absorbent requires expensive capital-intensive equipment. Technologists should investigate other possibilities. In the meantime, there seems to be no reason why women could not be employed in the assembly of sanitary towels, using ready-bleached cotton wool, and manually-operated machines to produce knitted tubular cotton sleeves.

5. OTHER PRODUCTIVE ACTIVITIES

Apart from manufacturing, a popular way of earning cash in rural areas is through growing vegetables or trees/shrubs/plants or rearing livestock and then selling these and their by-products in local markets. The types of activity involved include market gardening; fruit tree planting; tree nurseries; poultry rearing (for meat and eggs); beekeeping (for honey and beeswax); dairy farming; goat rearing (for meat and milk); rabbit rearing (for meat and fur); fish farming and crocodile farming.

Traditionally, gardening, tree care and the care of small animals (but not bees and fish) have been the responsibility of women, although such activities are usually aimed at supplementing the family diet, supplying the family with firewood and providing a reserve supply of wealth, rather than generating regular income.

In recent years, many projects have aimed at converting such household tasks into income-generating activities. By and large, the trend has tended to help rather than harm rural women, although there are one or two notable exceptions such as the 'white flood' programme in India. This famous, often-quoted programme was, at face value, a good thing. It involved the introduction of dairies in order to improve the production and distribution of pasteurized whole milk to urban areas. It reduced waste, cut down disease and improved the nutrition of poor people in urban areas. Unfortunately, poor women in rural areas have ended up worse off than they were before. Women of the poorer castes used to graze buffalo, seeking out marginal areas of grass. They would milk them, make butter and sell the fruits of their labour in a nearby town. They would keep the skimmed milk to feed their own families. Now all this has changed since the dairies handle the cattle, and the dairies are run by men. Thus the meagre but independent income the women used to earn has mostly disappeared. Poor families no longer get the benefits of buttermilk, which they received free; instead the women need cash to buy milk, but they have lost their capacity to earn it.

The experiences related in the case studies in this section tend to be more positive than this, although they do indicate the complex nature of implementing income-generating projects based on horticulture and husbandry. The projects are of three types: those which assist women to expand existing activities; those which enable women to gain access to activities hitherto denied to them for sociocultural or economic reasons; and those which introduce a totally new activity into an area. Which project falls into which category is determined much more by location and culture than by the nature of product. For example, in Bangladesh, the vegetable production programmes for women represent an extension or improvement of existing activity; in Botswana they represent the introduction of a new activity or product type.

Winter Vegetables in Bangladesh The Women's Development Programme (WDP) is an integrated rural development project which began working with the rural women of 90 villages of the Tangail District in 1980. It is run by CARE, a private development agency. One of the main activities implemented through the WDP is winter vegetable cultivation. In this project, high-quality seeds and seedlings of carrots, cabbage, radishes, tomatoes, cauliflowers and two types of local vegetables are distributed by CARE, and then cultivated by village women, with supervision by CARE field staff. The extension staff are mostly women with in-house training, who spend two or three days a week in each of the villages under their supervision.

The village women deposit money for the purchase of their seedlings in a village development fund—a communal fund held in a bank account which is operated jointly by a secretary who is a female leader elected by the village women, and CARE. As the fund accumulates, it may be used by village women for other self-help projects in their villages, such as purchasing poultry vaccination kits. In this way, women are given an extra incentive to cultivate vegetables without CARE actually supplying the seeds free of cost. Only village women, not men, are allowed to purchase seeds or seedlings in this programme.

After depositing their money and preparing their vegetable beds, the village women plant their seeds. Local government officials, as well as village women leaders selected by CARE, help in the organization of the project and in giving information on vegetable cultivation. At the same time, an intensive education campaign is mounted to give information on the techniques of vegetable cultivation. Three women from each village are given a five-day training course on the techniques of vegetable cultivation, both theoretical and practical, at the CARE offices. These women are encouraged to disseminate their knowledge to others and act as 'model farmers' in their villages. Additionally, the extension workers regularly give informal training at village level. These extension activities are supplemented by the establishment of village-level demonstration plots, primary school demonstration plots and simple, comprehensive handout sheets of cultivation instructions for trainers.

In the first year, 2,815 women from 60 villages were involved in vegetable production. Total production was about 500 tonnes—an average of 144 kg per participant. After production costs, this represented a net worth of TK 250. In most cases, some of the vegetables were retained for home consumption with the rest being sold. Radishes were a major contributor to income; but as was to be expected, the local leafy vegetables were not so popular as they had a low market value per maund (37.33 kg).

About two-thirds of the participants had been involved in growing vegetables before the project was introduced. Thus they had some knowledge or skill, but had not been able to produce such a wide range of vegetables. Many women were encouraged to bring small, previously vacant plots of land under cultivation as a result of the project.

An evaluation of the project yielded some interesting information. The participants were asked if they would like to make a co-operative garden, working with other women. All the respondents said they would prefer to cultivate their gardens individually. CARE staff had previously worked with women's co-operatives and did, indeed, find that most women would rather work alone: the problems of equitably sharing work and products was seldom easily resolved. Because of the small investment and limited size of the gardens, there is little incentive to pool resources into a co-operative.

After land preparation, women usually irrigate small plots themselves, carrying the water in earthenware pots. Most respondents (87 per cent) claimed they had irrigated their own plots. Where irrigation had not been carried out, the women maintained that it was not required. However, field workers felt that insufficient irrigation was a serious constraint on yield. Even fewer respondents (78 per cent) claimed to have erected a fence. Some said that cost was the inhibiting factor; others said there was no need because there were no animals to protect against, or because the plot was close enough to the household. At the beginning of the season, CARE became aware of serious damage to the vegetable plots from goats, chickens, children and other pests and predators because there was no fencing. By the end of the season—unfortunately not before considerable damage had been done—a significant number of respondents had erected fencing.

When asked if they had obtained the results they expected, the majority of participants (64 per cent) replied positively. Most respondents (98 per cent) also said that their neighbours, having seen their plots, were more interested than before in cultivating vegetables.

The most serious problem in the project was the absence of fencing. It was also noted in areas where poultry is reared intensively by free-range methods, that even a well-made fence was not sufficient to keep out chickens; they were frequently seen flying over metre-high fences to eat vegetables. The most successful plots were found in Hindu villages where no chickens or goats were kept.

Excessive shade was another problem. Many models for intensive household cultivation assumed that the household would be rationally planned so that buildings and trees would be placed to allow some areas to receive enough sunlight for gardening. This obviously is an unrealistic assumption: some household compounds have no sunny areas.

Theft is another major problem—one which is seldom acknowledged in the literature. Villagers sometimes relied on traditional measures, such as placing an amulet in the field. Extension workers asked all participants to encourage their neighbours to grow vegetables—the logic being that if everyone had a plot of their own, there would be less incentive to steal, although this hardly complements an income-generating strategy based on local markets.

This study shows how important it is to have female extension workers in a culture where men cannot communicate easily with women outside their immediate family.

Vegetable Co-operatives in Botswana The Mahalapye Development Trust Group in Botswana is part of the Brigades Movement which aims to provide practical job-oriented training to young people not going on to secondary school, and to provide a means of productive employment after training. The Brigades/Trusts are local, village-level, non-governmental organizations controlled by locally elected trustees.

One of the projects started by the Mahalapye Trust is co-operative commercial gardening. Co-operatives exist separately for men and for women. The majority of communal production projects tried elsewhere in Botswana have failed, but the arrangements made in Mahalapye seem to have worked. The projects were developed from the participants own ideas and stated needs. Thus, while men opted from the start to concentrate exclusively on vegetables for sale, the women chose to start with small plots, producing for home consumption. Only later, having gained confidence in a new activity without the pressures of financial failure, did they branch out into co-operative commercial production. Not all the women with individual plots went on to 'greater' things: those who did proceed were found to be, either heads of households, thus having greater need, or women with less demanding husbands, who therefore had more time available. Many husbands expected their wives to contribute labour to their own vegetable plots, thus denying women the chance of having their own income-generating plots. When women did move into co-operative commercial ventures, they were found to participate much better than the men.

In the case of co-operative ventures, participants had to raise 10 per cent of the capital costs themselves, with a donor agency providing the remainder as a grant. This was to cover external fencing, irrigation equipment, and other necessities. The groups consist of 10 people who farm individual plots of 1.5 ha. between them. There are no 'traditional' vegetables: produce includes crops such as carrots, cabbage and tomatoes.

Difficulties were experienced in timing the harvests of different vegetable crops so that they provided a continuous source of income. As a consequence, the incomes of most groups fluctuated considerably, with spells between harvest when there was no income. Another problem was that all the agricultural extension agents (who were essential to the

A women's vegetable co-operative in Africa.

scheme) were men. It was found that the male vegetable growers were better able to mix and communicate with such workers and were therefore more successful than the women at lobbying for support and resources. The volunteer expatriates working at the trust (also men) recognized this problem and adopted a policy of positive discrimination towards the women's groups, giving them encouragement and support. It was felt that the women's co-operatives might have failed without this support.

Bananas in Samoa Amaile village in the Aleipata district of Samoa is located 45 miles east of Apia and has a population of about 200.

When a development agency first discussed the idea of income-raising activities with the women in the village, they showed cynicism about the idea of a group project because they mistrusted one another. However, there were four women who were keen to start some kind of project and they decided to work together, irrespective of the others.

On the basis of resources available to them, the four women decided that a banana project would be the most feasible. One of the member's husband made some of his land available for the purpose and also allowed the women to make use of banana corms from an old plantation he wanted removed.

In order to acquire equipment, such as a spray gun, the women decided that they would have to raise funds. This they did by collecting coconuts each week, which were then sold as copra. They also held a dance in the village which the whole district attended for a minimal charge.

With the help of their families, the women started planting. The field officer of the agriculture department in their district was contacted to advise on care and maintenance of the plantation. It was established that selling the bananas in town would not be profitable due to high transport costs. Fortunately, the plantation is situated alongside the new access road into the district so that the women were able to sell their bananas to those commuting to and from Apia.

The benefits of the project have been most substantial. Each member has her own savings account into which profits go after maintenance money has been put aside. Two members are heads of household and are the sole breadwinners. Profit from the project has helped fund the starting of other projects, such as poultry- and cattle-rearing.

Through their efforts and success these four women have inspired other women in the village to start up similar income-earning projects. The women felt that it was easier to work in small groups to ensure maximum co-operation than if they were to join forces and work together as a single group. The other women find the idea of banana-growing attractive because of the high returns it brings. However, they do not have access to a sufficiently large area of land. Other types of project are being investigated.

It needs to be remembered that co-operation between individuals in villages is not an easily acceptable concept in some countries and cultures. Apart from this, there are three points worth noting: first, the way in which women raised their own money to buy inputs; second, the effect of demonstrable success in interesting other women; and third, the problem of marketing agricultural produce in remote communities with no access to transport. Selling by the roadside is one solution: processing/preserving as banana chips plus occasional trips to town could have been another, which would also have added value to the product.

Tree Planting in Kenya The National Council of Women in Kenya has created an active, rapid-growing and relatively successful tree planting programme. This was initiated in 1977. The objectives of this programme are not only energy related (fuel supplies), but are conservational as well, aimed as they are at countering the desertification process. The mature trees are also intended for multi-purpose use including commercial wood production. The programme has two major components (a) the Green Belt movement; and (b) tree nursery development. Both are carried out through local women's groups and are overseen by the Central Nairobi Office. Both components are carried out on a request basis. Local groups send in application forms for tree seedlings and the necessary tools. The Central Office responds to applications, co-ordinates the distribution and collection of seedlings, maintains central seed nurseries and keeps careful records of application forms and follow-up reports.

The Green Belt movement involves the planting of demonstration trees, primarily for conservation and environmental improvement. The projects generally involve a small number of trees planted on small areas of public land, but this is often done for commemorative or special occasions, as well. Although the local women's groups sponsor these Green Belt plantings, the planting itself does not usually involve their participation, although they may be concerned with tree maintenance thereafter. As of August 1982, there were over 200 new green belts in Kenya and the movement was rapidly expanding.

By comparison, the tree nursery component involves the full participation and active work of members at the local level. There are a larger number of trees per project and a cash incentive contract system. In this case, the purposes of tree-raising are multiple, with fuelwood being one of the intended end uses of the wood that is produced. The projects require labour by the women members to prepare tree nursery plots (often in a communal piece of land), plant seedlings and

A tree nursery in Kenya.

maintain them, using simple tools provided by the Central Office and, if necessary, acquiring technical assistance from the forest department officer in the local area. In cases where a communal plot is not available, the women may raise seedlings on their own farms. When seedlings are mature, the NCW central office purchases the seedlings from the women for 0.50 shillings (50 US cents) per seedling, so each individual woman receives cash payment for her labour and produce. The NCW attempts to give priority to requests coming from particularly needy areas when reallocating seedlings to other members of women's groups, farmers and other customers for planting. As of August 1982, there were over 50 NCW nurseries in Kenya, and this programme has been steadily expanding.

An evaluator of the nursery development scheme felt that the success of the project lay in the role that the women themselves play—they are in control of the projects including the management, decision making and physical work. Also, the women see the benefits of adopting an innovation which has the potential to ease burdens associated with their own activities (i.e. fuelwood collection). The cash payment for seedlings in particular creates an incentive to participate and to care for trees.

Poultry Keeping in Kenya In 1975, a group of 20 women decided to form a co-operative for keeping chickens. Each member contributed 700 shillings which she had saved from earnings doing casual farm labour. The land was a gift, but the buildings had cost 9,000 shillings and their 400 chickens another 2,020 shillings. Since the nearest water source was a river some 3.2 or 4.8 km away, they had also invested 500 shillings in a steel drum for storing water. After a year, it was decided that another container was needed, but in that short space of time their cost had risen to 800 shillings and the group could not afford the extra outlay. Chicken feed for 400 chicks is 436 shillings per week. In addition, 100 shillings per month is paid to one woman for looking after the chickens and 60 shillings per month is paid to a watchman. It was estimated that to break even, an egg would have to be sold for 40 cents. This compares with the local eggs which sell at 25 cents each.

At the request of the Women's Bureau, the Ministry of Agriculture carried out an analysis of the economics of poultry keeping and discovered that in the area in question, a minimum of 750 chickens would be needed. The Women's Bureau extended the loan to enable to group to expand their business.

This is a good example of why project initiators should work through the economics of various project activities before recommending them. The optimum size of operation will vary from place to place depending on local prices and circumstances and has to be calculated individually for every project. The tendency is to assume that economics are not a significant factor in women's projects: it needs to be impressed on all concerned that they are—especially if loans have to be repaid.

Poultry Raising in Bangladesh The Putitila Hindu Women's Group in the Roazon region of Bangladesh decided to raise chickens because they had been led to understand by a development agency working in the area that this would be a profitable venture. Food for the chickens was supplied by the women from left-overs and any wastes to hand.

Poultry raising and chicken-eating is forbidden to Hindus in this part of Bangladesh and the group's actions encountered immediate hostility from many religiously influential people. Despite this, they remained resolute, because of the pressing need for some source of income.

This case study poses an interesting sociocultural dilemma. Should women be encouraged to defy local customs and traditions in the interests of monetary gain? How far can this be done without becoming counter-productive?

Goats and Kids in South India Kerala's social welfare authorities have made the popular women's clubs found everywhere in the State the firm basis for their programme to improve family health and income. In at least half of the villages and rural districts of Kerala, the clubs, with the help of the State and voluntary agencies, have built a hut of bamboo and thatch, or found a large room for use as a day-care centre. These balwadis, as they are known, are staffed by mothers under the supervision of a local woman whom they select for basic training in home science, agriculture, nutrition and health care. Professional social workers oversee the 1,601 balwadis scattered throughout Kerala.

The balwadis are not just a place for mothers to leave their children during the day. Mothers help prepare food supplements for their children; health workers make regular visits to examine children and explain about sanitation; new practices such as the use of latrines are introduced. But the women of Kerala are poor and at this stage, they are far less interested in latrines than in earning money. Learning about ways to earn money is one of the main attractions of the centres.

It was through this need to provide balwadi women with income-generating projects that UNICEF engaged itself in goat rearing in Kerala. It finances a revolving fund enabling women's clubs to purchase young goats which are given to mothers to raise. When her goat has kids, she gives one to another mother, and so the chain goes on. She also gives milk to the balwadi kitchen and can use or sell the rest. In each balwadi, the women's club selects the first 10 mothers to receive a goat from among the poorest of the women who bring children to the centre. Since 1976, 10,000 mothers have benefitted from the programme.

Goat Rearing in Bangladesh Since 1977, a private agency in collaboration with the Bangladesh Government Integrated Rural Development Project (IRDP), has been running a programme to aid landless and women's co-operatives by giving starter fund loans. These loans are made available to individual members of the co-operatives as starting capital to enable them to undertake income-generating projects of their own choosing. The participants are required to pay back their loans in instalments. Most of the participants are widows, women separated from their husbands, or divorced women with no source of income. The loan is interest free: the maximum loan per member is TK 300. Loans are now being given to over 3,000 members per annum.

One of the more popular activities taken up in the early years of the scheme was goat raising which, on paper, is a highly profitable venture. However, in practice, loanees experienced

Rearing goats produces a source of income for Indian women.

many difficulties. In some cases, the goat died, creating extreme hardship for the project participant who was still required to pay back the loan. Technical support was not sufficient to keep goat mortality at a minimum. Further, since most of the profit from goat raising occurs only when the goat's kids have reached marketable age, beneficiaries may be faced with loan repayments before receiving any major source of income from the goat. Other recipients were disillusioned with goat raising because it required a steady outflow of cash but did not provide a steady flow of returns. All in all, goat-rearing ceased to be popular with loanees who preferred projects such as rice husking which gave a lower return on investment and had a low labour productivity but which had negligible risks associated with them while generating a steady income.

Beekeeping in Kenya With the help of a loan from the government Women's Bureau, a group of 35 rural women in Western Kenya established and are running a very successful beekeeping business.

Traditionally, beekeeping in Kenya, and elsewhere in Africa, is men's work, since collecting honey from wild bees requires climbing trees, an activity not normally undertaken by women. Obviously, in these circumstances, the women were not very interested in the idea of beekeeping when it was first suggested to them. They became more interested however when the Women's Bureau staff explained to them that some new beehives had been developed which gave higher yields of honey than traditional hives and which could be sited anywhere in the household compound. Interest was increased further when it was explained that a woman farmer in a nearby district was already successfully keeping bees with the use of these hives. The bureau arranged for two members of the group to visit the woman involved and when they returned they assured the rest of the group that the idea was one which should be acted on.

An extension officer from the Ministry of Agriculture was called in to give a training course and to help the women establish the project. He visited the group regularly during the

In many parts of the world, livestock provides women with a source of income.

early days to give advice and support. Most of the loan from the Women's Bureau was used on purchasing the 20 hives (which were made to order at the local village polytechnic) and the bees. Some was left over to buy additional equipment such as catcher boxes and smokers.

The women lost the bees in one hive due to infestation by red ants, but the others are giving a good yield, i.e. six bottles of honey from each harvest from each box. At four harvests a year and a price of 15 shillings per bottle, this is proving very profitable. (Compare with price of 85 shillings for a hive). At the moment, the agricultural extension officer undertakes the harvesting for the group because they have not been able to afford the expensive protective clothing needed to do this task. Once the loan to the Women's Bureau has been repaid, profits will be put towards the purchase of this clothing. In the meantime, the Women's Bureau has suggested to the local village polytechnic that some of the girls in the sewing class might be trained in production of these items, and helped to establish a small business producing them for sale to the growing number of beekeeping groups in the area. Supplies from a local business would be less expensive than the imported clothing currently being used.

A new addition is a simple solar wax extractor which the women were able to make themselves, with assistance from the carpentry instructor at the local village polytechnic, using a wood box, a debe can (4 litre tin container) and a piece of glass. A shelf made from the debe tin is placed inside the box. This has holes punched in it at its lower edge. The box is tilted by resting it on a large rock. The waste material left after boiling the content of the hives to extract liquid honey is placed on the shelf and left to heat in the sun. Liquid wax drips through the holes onto a piece of tin and solidifies into pure wax. All dirt pieces, bees, and other wastes are left behind on the upper shelf. The women heard about this device from their agricultural extension officer who was also responsible for getting the polytechnic instructor to help out. He has since told the women that the Ministry is investigating the potential for utilizing the substance which bees make to waterproof their hives. This is believed to be valuable for certain medicinal purposes and to sell at 300 shillings per kilo in Europe. The women are excited about this development.

Fish Farming in Kenya In the early 1970s in Kenya, an international agency funded a project to promote fish breeding; this was not followed up with information on salting and drying techniques. When the breeding ponds were drained, the local farmers were left with piles of rotting fish, since there was neither the refrigerated transport to take the fish to Nairobi, nor the knowledge of simple methods of preservation. To further complicate matters, the local people were not fish eaters.

It seems obvious enough that, until some solution can be found, women will be unable to make money from an activity if there is no local demand for the product, no way of getting the product to a market, and no method of preserving or storing the product.

Summary There are a number of general themes in this section which should be emphasized.

Horticulture and husbandry can be quite high-risk investments, with severe losses resulting from spoilage by pest infestation, animal or child damage, ant infestation, disease and theft. This would seem to weigh against them as a basis for income generation for poor families in areas where monitoring and support systems, such as on-going technical assistance and veterinary services cannot be guaranteed.

Such projects can be very problematical in areas where the intended participants have limited access to land and where the necessary services and inputs, such as water and pollen flowers, are not conveniently located. This may seem obvious, but often gets overlooked, especially the water issue—irrigating a vegetable plot or watering 500 chickens can put impossible strains on overworked women if they have to carry water over substantial distances.

Cultural practices and consumer preferences have to be considered before introducing projects of this sort. Many people in Africa do not eat fish, while thousands in India do not eat meat; in the latter case there are often taboos about rearing animals, even for sale to people outside the community.

Backward and forward linkages to other village-level industries seem to be virtually ignored in such projects. With the possible exception of beekeeping, there is little mention of the potential for village-level production of inputs such as fencing, animal pens and hutches, animal feed, fish cages and water storage containers. Nor is there any mention of village-level processing of commodities (except honey and wax). Value could be added to many commodities by processing them in various ways before sale—preserving vegetables; plucking chickens to make them oven-ready, as is done in Guyana with the help of a pedal-powered chicken plucker; dehydrating or smoking fish; and skinning rabbits.

Many projects seem to aim at introducing imported concepts into vegetables and livestock production, e.g. European vegetable varieties and rabbit breeds. Little is ever said about promotion of more indigenous activities such as crocodile farming which, in some countries, may be a more profitable investment.

6. SERVICES

Traditionally, women have offered a wide variety of services within the rural community, sometimes free of charge, but mostly for payment. Most villages have a traditional midwife, and traditional healers are also often women. Many women offer water or fuelwood collection and carrying services or operate crop processing businesses using traditional techniques. In most countries, women are involved in small retailing businesses and in parts of the world, such as West Africa, rural women earn income predominantly from marketing and trading operations. By and large, the work is hard—much of it involving carrying heavy loads over long distances on foot, or spending long hours processing crops with primitive tools—and the pay is very low indeed.

There are two major trends in the service sector. First, as rural incomes increase, a greater proportion of income is spent on services as opposed to food and manufactured goods, thus making it a growth sector. Also, as development proceeds, more machinery and equipment is introduced into the rural areas which demands new skills in operation, maintenance and repair. Second, as the nature of the service sector changes the women are, predictably, excluded and often displaced from employment by the change. Owners and operators of rural rice mills tend to be men as do pump mechanics and truck drivers, even though milling, water-drawing, lifting and transportation are traditionally female service activities.

The case studies in this section look at projects which have been aimed specifically at helping rural women to earn income through the provision of basic village-level services and thus share in the benefits of increasing demand for service activities. They fall into two major categories. First, the 'barefoot' variety of services following the model of the barefoot doctor example from Asia. The projects included are: barefoot veterinarians in Bangladesh; barefoot mechanics in Nepal and Bangladesh; and barefoot agriculturalists in The Gambia. Second, the 'custom' variety of services whereby the owner of a piece of equipment charges other people for its use. Custom-designed projects include running a rice mill in Bangladesh, hiring threshers and solar dryers in Bangladesh and running a bus service in Kenya.

Barefoot Vets in Bangladesh A private agency in Bangladesh has set up a system whereby village women learn how to vaccinate chickens. Women are trained in three day sessions held in regional towns and in local villages. The women thus trained then vaccinate all the birds in the village. In many villages, the women have used their own savings to purchase the necessary syringes, needles and flasks for vaccination so that the development agency no longer needs to supply any equipment. However, the agency's extension workers help the village women to organize monthly vaccinations so that village stock is constantly protected; gradually it is hoped that this activity will be completely taken over by the village women. The villagers pay 10 paisa (about half a cent US) per bird vaccinated so that the village immunizers are compensated for their time. The District Livestock Officers have been asked to try to distribute poultry vaccine to the village women who have been

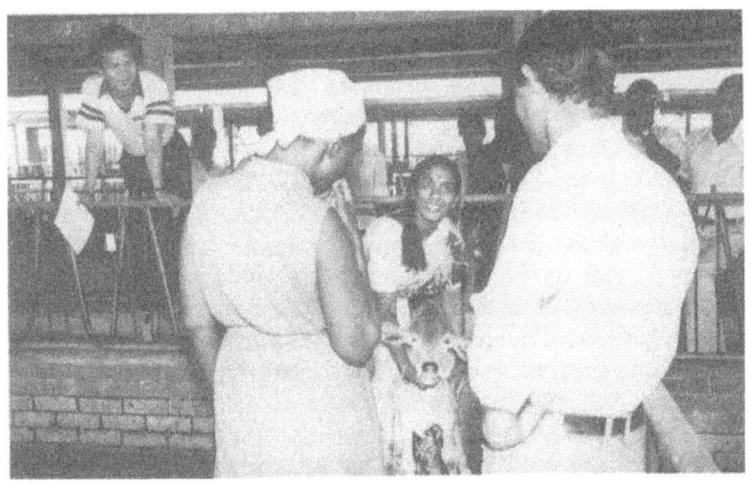

After training, women can earn income from caring for the village animals.

trained through this scheme. Although the DLOs were skeptical at first, they have now agreed to work with these village women.

The women trained are now vaccinating about 73,000 birds every four months and the development agency is slowly being able to withdraw its support. A major problem, still in need of solution, is maintaining the supply of vaccine and ensuring the cold chain is not broken. At present, the development agency staff get supplies from the Livestock Service in Dhaka for transport to the villages in insulated flasks.

This programme is run in conjunction with the agency's poultry farm which supplies improved breeds of birds to groups of poor women. It has greatly reduced the risks involved in poultry rearing through prevention against Newcastle and other common poultry diseases.

Barefoot Mechanics in Nepal and Bangladesh A much-quoted case study is that of a village water system in Lesotho which broke down after several years during which no maintenance had been undertaken. The maintenance committee, all women, tried but failed to get cash and/or labour contributions even though villagers spoke vociferously of the need for the water system. Women blamed the men for refusing to join work parties. The men said maintenance of the water supply was a job for women as women benefitted most from more accessible water. They also suggested that the women on the committee were incompetent.

In Nepal, similar water delivery systems, which piped water down the mountains, were constantly in disrepair. A Peace Corps project to teach women how to repair and maintain the pipes reportedly resulted in a much more effective system. Similarly a UNICEF project in Bangladesh has trained women in the maintenance and petty repair of village hand-pumps.

Barefoot Agriculturalists in The Gambia Having recognized the need for female staff to make inputs directly to women farmers and having failed to find any college-educated officers willing to live in the agricultural areas, a World Bank-financed project in The Gambia began identifying and recruiting female school leavers and training them in agricultural techniques. Having been brought up and educated in the area they were to work in, there seemed to be a good chance that these girls would be content to stay put.

These agricultural assistants were trained in a number of simple techniques, such as measuring out fertilizer correctly and accurately, which they could then teach to women farmers. Payment for their work came from the Government.

The belief that these women would remain in the local community proved to be a realistic one. There have been other problems, however. In particular, the women farmers have been slow in accepting the trainees as demonstrators. A recent evaluation of the project suggests that such reluctance is based on a healthy suspicion of the advice urged by young people, whether male or female, who have acquired their knowledge secondhand and have not tested out their prescriptions in a rigorous way in the real world. The solution to this problem was thought to lie in recruiting and training more mature women who are selected by their fellow villagers for their experience and appreciation of problems.

Millers in Bangladesh The Grameen Bank Project (GBP) in Bangladesh is specially designed to bring credit services within the reach of landless women who cannot offer collateral for bank loans. Loans are made to groups of five women. So far, a total of 2,101 women groups with a membership of 10,400 has been organized. Several groups in the same village are federated into a 'centre' which meets at a designated place for regular weekly meetings. Out of the group leaders a centre chief is elected.

One of these centre chiefs was interested in initiating a joint enterprise involving several groups. She attended several workshops and discussed the issue with other loanees and GBP workers. At one workshop, she was highly inspired by the success story of the Narandia Women's Association which had just set up the first all-women rice-husking mill. Thus enthused she set about persuading women in her own village to embark on a similar venture.

During the first few weeks of her campaign, most of her group members considered it an impractical proposition, but due to her ceaseless efforts and strong self-confidence, most members were eventually convinced. The bank workers concerned also laid stress on group-based activities and the idea gained more and more support. Eventually, 40 women (eight groups) contracted a loan of TK 24,000 from the GBP to set up a husking machine. The loan per capita was TK 600 and the rate of repayment was TK 12 per instalment.

The machine was installed in the yard of the group leader's house. The present machine shed was formerly a cow-shed. The group members made another shed for her cattle. All the members joined in the building of the shed and took a loan from their group fund to purchase necessary materials. They also broke about three tonnes of rock into small pebbles for flooring.

The group leader trained herself to operate the machine and in turn taught other members. There is an eight-member committee to keep account of the rice mill. Ordinary members participate in cleaning the machine house and in changing the water in the reservoir.

There was a simple ceremony to inaugurate the rice mill and, for promotional purposes, paddy was husked free of charge for the first two days.

The machine uses diesel fuel. The charge for husking 16 seers (1 seer = 0.933 kg) of paddy is TK 1.50. This rate was fixed in relation to the price of the diesel and the prices charged by other mills in the area. So far, the highest daily husking rate is 1,072 seers.

After setting up the mill, trade in paddy has received a boost in the neighbourhood. At present, there are four women who are full-time rice traders and their income has gone up. Local men also started to come to husk their rice here when the machine in the marketplace cannot be operated because of electricity failure. This happens very frequently, so demand for the service of the women's mill is increasing steadily.

Many of those who opposed setting up the mill in the beginning have now become patrons and clients. People from far off places also come to see the women-operated rice mill to assure themselves that such a thing is possible. It is raising new hopes, and even though it has not yet achieved break-even point, it is a source of inspiration to others.

Every week TK 480 must be paid back in bank instalments. In order to do this, over 1,000 seers of paddy must be husked every day. Although this target has been reached occasionally the average is currently only about a third of this. However, demand for the service is growing rapidly.

Custom Work in Bangladesh An interesting scheme run by some of the private agencies in Bangladesh is the granting of loans to small groups of landless women for the purchase of crop-processing equipment which they can then use to provide custom services to farmers in their area.

In the Comilla District, an experiment has been made with one group of women, who dry cabbages and other vegetables for local farmers on a contract basis, using a solar dryer. More widespread is the group ownership of pedal-operated threshers which are hired out (with operators) to farmers for threshing paddy harvests. The pedal thresher has enabled many more women to participate in the threshing operation, since it allows threshing to be carried out within the confines of the compound, rather than out in the open fields. Other devices still in the design stage, which could form the basis of this type of rural employment, include the back-pack huller which, if owned by a women's group, would enable them to earn income by offering custom services to the wives of wealthier farmers.

This is an interesting example of how women can put improved technologies to work for them rather than being displaced by them. Loans and training are necessary and in some cases, so is mobility. If mobility is restricted, solar drying of farmers crops at home is a good idea.

Logically, in areas where land preparation has been a women's task there seems to be no reason why women should not also be trained as tractor drivers so as to gain employment in widespread tractor hiring businesses to farmers. Women have already been trained in some African countries, such as Lesotho and Ghana.

Bus Service in Kenya The Taita women in Mraru raise large families, produce food for their families and earn what money

With the help of a loan women can buy machinery, such as a threshing machine, to work for local farmers.

they can from selling any surplus food and livestock and through petty trading at the market in nearby Voi.

In the early 1970s, drought conditions were making trading more important than ever, but all women in the area were having extreme difficulty in getting to Voi because of lack of transport facilities. Women were also anxious about the difficulties of getting sick children to the health centre in Voi. The idea arose with one women's group to buy a bus. It was agreed that each member, over time, should contribute at least 200 shillings, which would be the value of one share.

After 18 months, the group had saved 27,000 shillings and the group leader travelled to Mombasa to place an order for a bus with the Cooper Motor Corporation. Here it was found that a 21-seater bus would cost 111,780 shillings and that a down payment of 47,800 shillings would be needed before a bus could be released. The process of securing the extra money for the down payment and persuading a credit bank in Nairobi to give a loan to cover the rest of the purchase price was tortuous but successful and, five years after the idea had arisen, the bus arrived in Mraru.

The Mraru women now had a full-scale business on their hands. They had insurance and registration fees to pay, they had to buy petrol and pay for maintenance and they had to meet a monthly debt repayment of 4,088 shillings over 18 months. In addition, they had three full-time employees—the driver, the conductor and an inspector. At first a woman was hired as conductor, but customers were sometimes too rowdy for her to handle so a young man was appointed instead. The inspector is always a member of the woman's group.

Each passenger pays 3 shillings for the one-way, 12-km trip from Mraru to Voi. A day's gross for the bus service varies from 120 to 800 shillings; on market days and holidays it can reach several thousand. The bus is also available to hire for special trips such as school outings.

The bus proved an excellent investment. In a year and a half, the debts were paid off and the group began a new savings account. After a few months, they had 12,000 shillings in the bank and were accumulating more all the time. The group then declared half the money as a dividend and targeted the remaining funds for a new enterprise, a retail shop in Mraru. News of the success spread quickly. At the time of the issue of the dividend, the group had 68 members; two years later the number had grown to 195. The shop does a steady business although it is nowhere near as profitable as the bus.

Not surprisingly, given heavy use, by the time the bus was four and a half years old, repair bills began to equal earnings and the group decided it was time to turn the machine in for a new one. The manufacturers were willing to give a good trade-in price (60,000 shillings) and the group had 31,600 shillings in savings above that. However, inflation had raised the price of a new bus from 111,000 shillings to 310,000 shillings and a suitable loan to cover this could not be arranged. The women wondered for the first time if they should have saved up for a new bus rather than investing in a retail store. With the bus not running, women began to experience the old problems of not being able to get to Voi. There was a need to raise much more capital to pay a deposit of 150,000 shillings on a new bus, but their main source of income, which came from the bus service, had ceased to exist.

The lesson about loans and investment of funds is a useful one. The requirements for loans on the bus were very strict and a loan was not given until the Bank was certain that repayments could be made. The terms of the loan for the retail store were not so stringent—perhaps if they had been, the women would have been unable to invest in such a low return investment and would still have had enough savings for a new bus.

Summary There clearly need to be more examples of experiences of women's involvement in rural service activities before generalizations can be made. For the moment, it would appear that custom work brings in more income, or should do, than the barefoot and maintenance type of activity. However, if one is really looking to the future, the need for village technicians is clearly going to rise significantly with the arrival in more village areas of electricity and piped water connections and the introduction of more machines and equipment in need of maintenance and repair.

Village life is changing and if women are to share in the benefits, rather than lose out, attitudes towards their participation in these various service activities need some serious re-shaping.

CHAPTER III

Progress Through Learning

1. GENERAL OVERVIEW

It is encouraging to find that so many case studies and evaluation reports on non-handicraft income-generating projects exist. The data they provide enable the factors, common to successful project design and implementation, to be isolated. However, the survey has also revealed a number of much wider issues which have some important and far-reaching implications for those involved in planning rural employment strategies.

First, it shows that the effort being put into employment creation for rural women consists primarily of small, isolated projects which, even when successful, benefit only a handful of women. Such projects are, of course, essential in demonstrating what sorts of work women can undertake to earn cash; but they will be of limited use unless they are widely replicated. Modernization and mechanization are displacing millions of women from paid employment as entire 'women's industries' are wiped out. As change occurs, there seem to be no new women's industries taking their place with the exception, perhaps of the put-out or dispersed factory systems in India, not all of which are as positive in their impact on women as the Lijjat enterprise described in Chapter II.

Second, the range of projects is not as varied as might have been hoped for; this indicates a lack of imagination on the part of project directors when selecting 'suitable' income-generating activities for women.

The projects tend to concentrate on food processing, clothing, fibre, horticulture and livestock. Few relate to shelter or to basic consumer goods, other than food and clothing. Of greatest significance is the total absence of case studies relating to producer goods manufactured by women. Although women have always been engaged in some way in the production of the tools and equipment they use to carry out their traditional tasks, it seems that the new generation of development practitioners sees them as only users and not also as manufacturers of these tools. This is a point which needs some emphasis and expansion since there is an enormous demand for producer goods in village communities, relating mainly to the production and processing of food and clothing and the provision of basic necessities such as shelter and water. These include hoes, ox-ploughs, rakes, jab-planters, bush knives, threshers, maize shellers, oil presses, grain mills, solar dryers, animal hutches, beehives, hand-pumps, irrigation channels, water pipes, spinning machines, looms, fibre decorticators, brick moulds, kick-wheels, carts, wheelbarrows, saws and hammers. Of these, reference was found only to the production of solar dryers by women: several groups in Guyana, Kenya and Tanzania have been taught the skills needed for production but little information is available as to fate of the groups after training.

Two trends seem to be behind this absence of activity. One is that as producer goods become more 'sophisticated' in nature—partly as a result of the need to increase productivity in agriculture and rural industry—the tendency is for the manufacturing base to be moved away from the village and towards more capital-intensive units in towns, cities or overseas. The other is, that while a great deal of effort goes into protecting and assisting village-level producer goods industries, little attention seems to be given to ensuring that women, as well as men, are involved in such initiatives. Thus, while women used to be involved in producing winnowing equipment from woven fibres, grating equipment from pieces of perforated metal, and transport equipment from woven fibres, bamboo and leather, they seem to be excluded from the production of 'improved' replacements such as pedal-operated winnowers (metal and wood), hand-operated coconut graters (metal and wood) and wheelbarrows, hand-carts and other transportation devices (normally metal and wood).

In most of Africa, women use agricultural tools, but are not taught to make them.

Part of the problem, of course, is that metal-working and wood-working are not normally thought of as women's work. Yet traditionally, blacksmithy and carpentry in most countries is a family business, with women fully engaged alongside their men—hence the often quoted example of village women in India hammering out bits of metal to make agricultural tools. Why then, should only men be involved in the production of the 'improved' equipment? Experience certainly suggests that if they are given the necessary training, women can be just as good at welding, carpentry and metal-working. Another very valid reason for having women included in the manufacture of producer goods is that very often it is women who are the users of such goods. Good notice should be taken of the example in Chapter II of stove-making in the Sahel, which shows that women users preferred the stoves made by women to those made by men and, in fact, stopped using the latter. It makes sense that women, who spend their whole lives in digging, planting and weeding, processing crops, preserving food and collecting and carrying water, firewood and other commodities, should have a better feel for adapting equipment used in these tasks to specific needs and preferences, than do men. Is it possible that more village-level innovations would have taken place in crop processing equipment if there had been more women blacksmiths and carpenters trained? Certainly evidence from the Sahel suggests that wood-saving stoves would be more widely in use by now if a start had been made sooner in teaching women artisans the basic scientific principles of improved stove-making.

Finally, there is little evidence of any 'depth' or vertical integration in the planning of women's income-generating activities. Only one or two projects have successfully included women in the various processes/stages of an industry, but none seem to follow through all the possible forward and backward linkages. For example, the soap-making project in Ghana relates back to women's groups making caustic potash, but does not go as far as linking up with other women's groups making bricks for the kilns which make the potash. The

Women should be thought of not just as users of technology but also as producers: these women in Guyana are being taught to make their own solar driers.

coconut dehydration project in Bangladesh sends coconut powder to biscuit factories in Dhaka, rather than forming the basis of the raw material for other women's groups making confectionary in nearby areas. The sort of industrial model which needs to be evolved, is that being attempted with the women coir workers in Sri Lanka, where one group of women purchases coconuts and, after retting, sells them on to another group who husks them. These then go to a third group of women who spin the fibre into rope. A fourth group then dye the rope, and yet another makes the ropes into coir mats. Only by bringing more and more productive activities into the rural areas, through backward and forward linkages, will it be possible to increase productivity and returns to labour in existing occupations, while maintaining levels of employment within the industry.

Having raised these wider issues—and bearing in mind that successful project design and implementation is a necessary, but not sufficient condition for the creation of rural employment opportunities on the scale needed—the rest of this chapter reviews the major factors in the success and failure of the various income-generating projects included in the report.

2. FACTORS IN SUCCESS . . . AND PROBLEMS

At the point where pilot projects are actually implemented, several factors can be clearly identified as bearing on the success of a project in meeting its objectives. Some of these obviously overlap, but for the sake of convenience (and clarity), they are dealt with individually and in no particular order of priority.

Raw Materials As might be expected, raw materials/input availability figures predominantly in the life of many projects. To a certain extent, those projects based on locally available materials are problem-free—but not always so. For example, in cases where a processing activity has been upgraded through the introduction of improved technology (fish-smoking and gari-making in Ghana; wool-spinning in India), supplies of the raw material may fall short of the increased demand if no plans have been made to ensure a complementary increase in production. Problems of this type can sometimes be overcome, either by involving other women's groups in production of the raw material, or (as in the Ghana cassava-processing example) encouraging men's co-operatives to commence or increase production.

The most critical problems were found in those cases where raw materials were available locally, but had a higher priority use in other parts of the economy; or where they were not available locally so that supplies depended on imports. Thus local supplies of coconut oil for soap-making in Tanzania and local supplies of palm oil for soap-making in Ghana were extremely scarce when most of the crop was needed to make cooking oil, leaving little surplus for secondary uses such as soap. In Tanzania the situation was simply accepted, with the soap co-operative working sporadically and well below capacity. In the Ghana case, however, local technological expertise is being used to try to solve the problem, while, at the same time, creating employment for more women, in the cultivation and processing of alternative oil-bearing seeds and fruits. Overcoming disruptions in supplies of imported raw materials can be much more difficult. For example, little could be done about the stoppage of weaving projects in Ghana when imported yarn became unavailable. By contrast, the tie-dye co-operative in Tanzania could possibly have survived if another co-operative had been established to produce dyes from local vegetation. This has been done successfully in other African countries such as Nigeria, following import bans on commodities such as dyes.

Thus, when planning income-generating projects for women, several questions relating to raw materials, need to be raised. What quantities are available and when? Who has control over the supply of raw materials. Can supplies be increased easily to meet an increase in demand? Will further projects be needed to enable increased output of raw materials? Are there competing uses for raw materials which could affect price and supplies? How easy would it be to find a substitute input if supplies of the raw materials became scarce or unavailable? Could extra rural employment be created by enabling women's groups to establish projects for manufacture/production of raw materials needed by other women?

Markets/Quality Control   Since one of the criteria for choosing projects was that they should be providing goods and services which were aimed at the local market, failures, due to lack of market demand, should have been relatively few.

Unfortunately, problems in selling products and services seemed to arise for a number of reasons. The most common of these was the failure to carry out a full market feasibility study before starting production. The result was that products could not be sold because, for example: the small market became quickly flooded (textiles in Swaziland); the product was not in a form the consumer wanted (mango purée in Honduras); or the product could not compete price-wise with competitors (ground spices in Bangladesh, eggs in Kenya).

Another problem that arose, especially with food processing projects, was poor quality of finished product (e.g. coconut powder in Bangladesh).

Of interest is the enormous range of marketing techniques in evidence in the projects. These vary from introductory offers made by the women's group themselves (rice milling in Bangladesh), through guarantees of quality by an established and respected technological institution (patenting of baby food in India) and display at national or international trade fairs (baby food in India), to lobbying of local institutions to support local industry (bread and school uniforms in Bangladesh) and arranging for bulk purchase in supermarkets in nearby towns (banana chips in Papua New Guinea).

Generally speaking, the marketing strategy seems to become more elaborate, with greater inputs being needed by outside agencies, as markets become less and less local. The extreme case of reliance on others for access to markets comes in those societies where institutions or private traders totally control the industry in the sense of supplying/selling raw materials and taking/purchasing back finished goods for retail sale. Although marketing problems are taken care of in such a system, the workers are all too often exploited (fishnet-makers in India, rope-makers in Sri Lanka, gatherers of traditional herbs in India), unless some way can be found to ensure that the people doing the work receive a just return for their labour. Pappad rolling, fishnet-making and traditional medicine in India, and coir workers in Sri Lanka, all represent varying attempts to help rural women workers by this means. Great care has to be taken in the case of existing industries not to make matters worse by stirring up resentment among private traders who are seeking to protect their vested interests. For example, the women coir workers in Sri Lanka will hardly benefit from being released from the grip of the market traders if this results in their supply of raw materials being cut off. Similarly, women who have been persuaded to rely on a voluntary agency for raw materials and access to markets may find it difficult to re-establish links with private traders if and when the voluntary agency withdraws.

Obviously, projects which have had the least marketing problems are those which fill a clearly defined gap—possibly caused by a ban on import of consumer goods (coconut sweets in Guyana; soap in many African countries), or by the expense of existing imported/urban produced products in relation to rural incomes (traditional medicine in India).

Again, project directors need to ask several questions about markets and quality. Are local markets available and are they seasonal or permanent? Are markets for certain products increasing or declining? What is the price and quality of existing competing products. Are there any standards with regard to taste, packaging or size, which need to be fulfilled so as to meet consumer preferences? Are there constraints, such as preference for imported goods, to contend with, and are there ways of overcoming these? Can markets be found through contacting government officials, schools, hospitals, supermarkets, or other organizations?

Can forward linkages be developed so that markets are created by supplying produce to other women's groups involved in productive activities? Can the product be made more competitive by the introduction of improved technology?

Commercialization A related, but somewhat different issue is that of commercialization. There are two aspects to this. First, most projects exhibit a somewhat welfare, institutional or non-commercial approach to marketing. Sales outside the immediate neighbourhood are often dependent on special arrangements made by external agencies or on special sales outlets. If goods do enter into the world of free enterprise, then it is normally the traders who are in control, with the result that production workers do not get a fair share of profits. Only one example (Lijjat pappads) is given of how use can be made of existing commercial channels (marketing agents), to sell a product while ensuring that distribution of profits stays in the hands of the producer. Many small firms in Asia employ marketing/sales agents on a full-time or part-time basis to bring in business and to look after their interests in areas in which they are not located. There seems to be no reason why women's groups/enterprises could not employ a similar strategy.

Second, in those cases where a new prototype machine is being developed for use by women's groups (oil presses in West Africa, coconut graters in Guyana, spice grinders in Bangladesh, ceramic stove liners in Indonesia), surprisingly little thought seems to go into establishing how such items will be commercially produced should demand be generated for them during the prototype testing phase. Most project directors tend to concentrate on having prototypes designed, developed and tested. They then assume that what happens thereafter is no concern of theirs and will be looked after by some other agency or will follow on automatically. However, as some of the case studies show, the issue is fraught with difficulties. Prototypes are often built by university engineering departments which have no capacity to go into commercial production and may have no time to devote to transferring the technology to commercial firms, or any interest in doing so. Commercial firms may have no capacity to do R & D work and may be disinclined to invest resources in setting up production of a new item for which demand (rather than need) is uncertain. If the R & D work was not done by the entrepreneur, he/she may also be reluctant to start up manufacture since the holder of the patent could easily allow other firms to enter the market, thus making production less profitable than initially anticipated. On the other hand, if a private firm holds the patent, a monopoly position can arise in which the price of the product is higher than it would be in a competitive market (e.g. the price of the Guyana coconut scraper would probably be less if there was some competition). Probably the best solution is for a neutral agency (e.g. a technology institute or a women's organization) to hold the patent so that both the incentive to produce, and also fair prices, can be maintained.

When planning ways in which various producer goods can be made available, it should not be forgotten that women as well as men can be involved in production. Women have been effectively involved in the production of solar dryers and solar wax extractors in various countries and there seems to be no reason why they could not set up enterprises to produce these and other producer goods on a commercial basis.

Many important questions need to be asked here. Can existing commercial channels (e.g. marketing agents) be used to sell products on a widespread basis? To what extent can commercial firms be expected to undertake production and distribution of tools and equipment needed by women's groups? What inputs might be necessary (loans, training, subsidies, demonstration projects) to encourage and enable commercial enterprises to start making new products for uncertain markets?

Credit/Loans The scarcity of cash in rural households is of particular relevance to women in rural areas who may have less opportunity to earn, and less control over their earnings than men. Thus, several case studies make reference to the uncertainties faced by women in projects which aim to sell them new goods, services or technologies (e.g. coconut graters in Guyana, ceramic stove liners in Indonesia).

Ways around the lack of cash problem vary with the amount of cash concerned. When only a few pence are involved (e.g. ceramic stove liners), the best strategy may be a total subsidization of a widespread testing phase to prove the economic worth of the product and persuade rural households (men and women) to invest scarce cash in this, rather than some other product or service. Trying to collect back hundreds of thousands of loans of this size would be more trouble than it was worth. However, where something of the pricing level of a coconut grater is concerned, it begins to be feasible to expect women to pay back in instalments once they start earning: thus enabling grants or loans to be recycled to other women/women's groups.

Most of the income-generating projects in the survey were based on some sort of loan facility or scheme: very rarely were women able to raise all the cash they needed to launch themselves into a business (the bakery project in Kenya and the banana project in Samoa are two instances in which they did), and obviously, the greater the investment, the larger the loan needs to be. For really big investments in such capital equipment as a bus, a grinding mill or a small-scale soap plant, some sort of co-operative structure will be almost essential in acquiring a loan.

Whether the loans are small individual ones or larger co-operative/group ones, the case studies point out the need for ensuring project feasibility so that loans can be repaid. Borrowing conditions may seem harsh at times (in terms of size of deposit, for example), but they can often prevent unwise investment decisions being made (e.g. the Mraru bus service and retail shop in Kenya). Loans need to be accompanied by investment advice and by necessary support services (training, technical back-up) to ensure that projects stand a chance of succeeding and that loans are more likely to be repaid. For example, goat-rearing projects in Bangladesh would have been less of a risk if backed up by veterinary services: certainly poultry projects there became a better risk after the introduction of the 'barefoot vet' scheme for vaccinating chickens. Such back-up services in the form of barefoot vets, barefoot mechanics and barefoot agriculturalists can create employment for some rural women, at the same time as reducing risks on investment for others.

The questions that should be asked are: what type and size of loan/credit facilities will be needed by women's groups. Are these available through normal lending channels? Can existing loan facilities be modified to accommodate the special needs and constraints of women or will special facilities be required? What conditions should be imposed upon women/women's groups taking out loans? What sort of back-up services need to be provided with loans to ensure successful investment and repayment?

Organization As with previous surveys of income-generating activities for women, it was found that the way in which production was organized—individual household, informal or formal group/co-operative, small enterprise, dispersed factory system—was an important element in project design and implementation.

By and large, it would be difficult to disagree with previous conclusions that some sort of group formation is the most appropriate form of organization. However, several projects reveal that women are not always immediately enthusiastic about co-operating (e.g. vegetable-growing in Bangladesh, biscuit-making in Honduras and banana-growing in Samoa). In addition, it needs to be remembered that while co-operation may make economic sense, other factors such as socio-cultural or legal constraints may make it impracticable. For example, land tenure systems may make co-operative vegetable projects impossible in parts of some countries (e.g. Bangladesh).

Thus, before starting a project it is important to ask how it should be organized—individual household production; informal groups, formal groups/co-operatives; dispersed factory system? What are the advantages and disadvantages of each under local conditions? Are there any types of project/product which should be rejected because they necessitate an organization structure which has more disadvantages than advantages?

Technology The adaptation/development and introduction of improved technologies comes out clearly as an important element of income-generating activities: some sort of new tool or technique seems to be involved in almost every project in the survey. Some of the issues raised by the case studies include: (a) the technology or technique is more likely to be accepted if it closely resembles existing technologies and does not necessitate any significant changes in skills, consumer preferences or cultural mores: (b) it is more likely to succeed if women are consulted during the design stage and if technologists fully investigate traditional processes during the design phase; (c) it is more likely to reach the potential beneficiaries (i.e. poor rural women) if there is a good working relationship between a technology institute and a women's organization.

There are technology centres in most countries/regions. The case studies from countries such as Ghana, Mali and Guyana show how these can successfully be put to work to assist rural women if the appropriate links can be formed between them and rural women, through national women's organizations.

Thus, if a technological improvement is necessary to a project, the project director needs to consider what measures should be taken to ensure that it is appropriate to the needs of rural women. Can women be easily included in the design of new technologies? Are there engineers who are willing to collaborate with women's organizations and visit rural areas to study existing processes undertaken by women?

Training, Extension, Monitoring   The nature, source and degree of training, extension and monitoring available was found to be important in many projects.

By and large, skills training or technical training seemed to be more readily available than marketing or business training. Lack of access to the latter had serious consequences for some projects (e.g. roofing sheets in Kenya, tie-dye in Tanzania) and caused constraints in others (day care furniture in Jamaica) until included in training. Given that we are dealing with income-generating activities, this lack of attention to basic financial business skills seems to be a serious oversight—arising perhaps from a perception of women's involvement in productive activity as a project in need of institutional support for bookkeeping, marketing and other similar inputs, rather than as a small enterprise in its own right.

As for the technical training, much of this seems to take

place outside the village environment, thus necessitating the mobility of one or two women and their ability to pass on skills to others after training. In countries/cultures where mobility is a problem, especially if lengthy visits away from home are required, this sort of system can put women at a disadvantage and alternatives may be needed, such as those designed for the Bangladesh vegetable gardening and barefoot vet schemes, whereby small groups of women are trained within their community.

As for the transfer of skills to other women after training, the projects show that this is something which women are really very good at, even if the skills are being transferred across country borders (Gambia to Mali). The success rate seems to depend on who is trained, how long the training lasts, how complicated the new technique is and how accessible follow-up training (out of village) or monitoring (on-the-job advice) turns out to be, and who is responsible for giving this. On the whole, it seems that success is more likely if the initial trainees are selected by the group, from within the group, and are thus well respected by the others. In cases where this was not done (e.g. roof sheets in Kenya (one expatriate and one man were trained); barefoot agriculturalists in The Gambia (young inexperienced schoolgirl leavers were trained), transfer of skills has not proved very effective. Length of training and the nature of the skill are obviously related and, generally, the more complicated the skill, the longer the training should be. In some cases (roof sheets in Kenya) the length of training has been clearly inadequate and, in this particular case, no follow-up training (either in or out of the village) was immediately available. Queries always arise when trying to put training into practice and in this case it is useful to be able either to return to the training centre (bakery in Kenya), or else to consult with qualified extension staff working in the village.

In this latter respect, the case studies point out the absolute necessity of having female extension workers in some countries or culture groups (e.g. Bangladesh) and the desirability of having some in many others (e.g. vegetable co-operatives in Botswana). Substantial inputs of time seem to be required from extension workers in the villages themselves, especially when new technologies/techniques are being introduced. Many of the voluntary agencies or small government agencies (e.g. women's bureaux) involved in income-generating activities cannot supply the necessary monitoring/back-up services from their own limited resources: those which have succeeded are the ones which have successfully acted as a catalyst in drawing on the more extensive resources of other agencies in the country (mainly governmental) and putting these to work for women (e.g. women's bureaux in Jamaica and Kenya).

The questions to be asked in relation to training include: what type of skills training and business training needs to be provided for different types of projects? What facilities exist or are needed to ensure proper provision of such training? Can women leave their villages to undertake training outside, or does it need to be provided within the village? Should all group members be trained, or only some, and how should selection be made? Do facilities exist to give on-the-job training and to monitor progress? Can use be made of government extension workers or do special arrangements need to be made and additional extension agents/demonstrators recruited? Are there any female extension agents: are they needed to ensure the success of the project? To what extent can employment be created for rural women as 'barefoot' extension agents?

Time Constraints An important issue raised by some of the case studies is that of the time constraints on women's involvement in income-earning activities. This came out particularly clearly in the wool-spinning project in India and in the vegetable co-operative in Botswana, where women often could not take advantage of a new technology/scheme simply because they were too busy with subsistence activities and, additionally, in the Botswana case, with assisting their husbands to earn cash through new income-generating ventures. In overlooking timing constraints, women are often advised to undertake income-generating activities of the most-time consuming variety (e.g. poultry rearing or vegetable gardening in areas of water scarcity) rather than those (e.g. rabbit rearing) which depend less on inputs of time for the same added value.

Given the time constraints on rural women, which restrict them in nearly all projects to fairly limited participation and often deny them the opportunity of fully exploiting the productivity increases of new technologies, it is disappointing to see that so few of the income-generating projects for women have been aimed at the production of labour-saving devices—thus killing two birds with one stone. If all women are involved in production of consumer goods then incomes will rise, albeit on a limited scale, due to the restricted hours available for such work. If some were involved in the production of labour-saving devices/technologies/products, then this could form the basis for a more substantial improvement in the village economy. There is little doubt that there would be a demand from women for such a strategy: the tree nursery scheme in Kenya was successful partly because women could identify this work with their own needs for firewood; and packaged caustic potash has proved popular with village women in Ghana as a labour- and money-saving device. More projects of this type are needed: for example involvement of women in the production of fuel briquettes from agricultural waste and the involvement of women in the production of various types of crop processing, transportation and water drawing/distribution systems.

In this case, the project director needs to ask such questions as: will women have time to participate fully in a new income-generating project, or to derive the full benefits of a more productive device? Is there a need for the introduction of labour-saving devices before women can participate in certain types of time-consuming income-generating activities? Is it possible to increase women's access to such technologies prior to the introduction of income-generating activities or do women first need to earn some cash (presumably from part-time work) so as to pay for labour-saving devices? To what extent can rural women be employed in the production of labour-saving devices and products?

Socio-Cultural Constraints   All projects involve changes, some of which may be more culturally acceptable than others. Many of the case studies point out the importance of being aware of existing traditions and particularly relationships between and within households in a community.

In some countries, resistance from men to the idea of women earning more income of their own seems common. Projects such as sericulture in Bangladesh and biscuit-making in Honduras show that this can be overcome if care is taken to include men in discussions relating to project implementation. Those projects which stand a better chance of success seem to be those in which the men also stand to gain, e.g. bottling vegetables in Honduras, where the women's activity enabled men farmers to reduce crop wastage.

Care obviously needs to be taken when introducing activities which are not normally thought of within the community as being women's work.

Several projects show, however, that women's non-involvement in certain types of activity is based more on a lack of experimentation or habit than any strong socio-cultural beliefs and that a single demonstration project can set off a whole new trend. This is shown for example with beekeeping in Kenya, milling and barefoot vets in Bangladesh and welders and carpenters in Jamaica. In other cases, women's non-involvement in certain activities may be a result of taboos and cultural beliefs in which case attempts to introduce change could be counterproductive. However, technological changes can sometimes overcome such problems, as with the introduction of broadloom weaving in Ghana.

Obviously, when planning a project, it is important to know whether there are certain types which are likely to run into problems because of resistance from husbands or the community as a whole. Are there ways in which such resistance can be overcome? To what extent are ideas about women's work founded on deep-rooted taboos and traditions which cannot (should not?) be broken, and to what extent are they based on less serious constraints, such as lack of precedence or lack of training facilities for women in certain crafts?

Economics of Production Possibly because women's income-generating activities are seen as part-time, little or no attention seems to be given to working out normal economic parameters, such as optimum size of unit, break-even point, profit margin and expected rate of return on investment. As was noted earlier, this can be a problem in cases where loans have to be repaid in regular instalments.

There would seem to be a need for more professionalism in establishing women's economic projects so that they stand a better chance of meeting women's need for income. Flow of income throughout the year should also be more widely considered, given women's need for cash on a regular basis. As was seen, women have rejected certain activities (goat-rearing in Bangladesh, market-gardening in Mali) which did not offer an immediate and year-round source of income. However, women's best interests may not always be served by opting for the low-risk, low-return, even-cash-flow activities. Careful planning such as that seen in the carpet-weaving project in Iran and the mango-purée project in Honduras can enable women to have confident access to higher return investments by introducing schemes for issue of cash in advance of sales, or by diversifying production to make use of idle capacity during off-peak agricultural seasons.

Before initiating any income-generating activity it is obviously important to make sure that the economics of the project been worked out properly. Is the optimum size of operation in relation to existing conditions and circumstances known? Does economic viability require full-time operation or is part-time work possible? If the former, can women accommodate this? Are there factors such as frequent shortages of inputs which might affect the project's ability to work at capacity?

Self-reliance/Agency Participation   The vast majority of projects in the survey exhibit a marked reliance on external agencies (indigenous and foreign NGOs, government departments) for their set-up and continued operation. By and large, women in Africa and the South Pacific seem to be much more likely to take initiatives in respect of raising cash to invest in projects than do women in Asia. This could possibly be because of their greater mobility and therefore greater access to casual employment opportunities which enables some money to be saved.

However, there are cases of independent initiative/activity

in Asia (milling in Bangladesh) and of extreme dependency in Africa (bakery in Botswana) and it would seem that the degree of reliance of a women's group on a support agency is perhaps due more to methodology/attitude of the agency than to sociocultural conditions in the area of operation. By and large, development agencies have a social welfare attitude towards women's groups, which tends to support and protect them from the real world, thus encouraging dependence rather than economic self-reliance.

It would seem important that project directors should assess the extent to which a potential project could expect to eventually become self-reliant. Are there some types of project which demand less outside inputs than others? What steps can be taken to reduce dependence on outside agencies?

Links between Projects There is a disappointing tendency for attitudes towards employment creation for rural women to be project-oriented as opposed to programme-oriented in the sense of trying to build up 'mini-industrial' systems within regions (whereby various projects relate to each other), or of trying to establish viable women's industries to take the place of those, such as rice-milling or beer-brewing which are being displaced by modernization and mechanization.

Some evidence is available of attempts to create women's employment through backward and forward linkages (e.g. soap, caustic potash and castor oil in Ghana; fruit processing and planting of fruit trees in Honduras; poultry rearing and barefoot vets in Bangladesh; beekeeping and making of solar wax extractors and protective clothing in Kenya), but much more needs to be done in this respect, especially in ensuring that women, as well as men, are included in those processes/types of production which exhibit the highest added value.

Less evidence is available of successful attempts to create new (or upgraded traditional) rural industries for women. For example, there are individual bakery projects owned by women in many villages but it has by no means become a widespread phenomenon in the sense that every village in the country has a bakery. Similarly, while there may be one or two women-owned and staffed rice mills in Bangladesh, a significant contribution towards provision of employment and income is unlikely to happen unless the few demonstration projects are replicated in villages throughout the country.

Thus, when designing projects, it is important to examine whether all possible backward and forward linkages have been explored in respect of providing employment opportunities for rural women. Are there bottlenecks on supply of raw materials or access to markets which could be broken by establishing another women's group in production? What are the possibilities of replicating successful projects in villages throughout a country? What measures need to be taken to assist in this process?

Government Policy Little attention seems to be given to the likely implications of changes in government policy for women's income-generating projects, and there is little evidence of attempts being made to help women to benefit from existing policy measures in support of small industries, or to bring about policy changes which will assist in achieving the aim of creating employment for women.

Permission given by a Government to construct a large modern bakery or a fruit/vegetable cannery could wipe out hundreds of small women's projects/enterprises overnight. Developments of this type happen very frequently, yet there rarely seems to be any effort made on the part of project managers to investigate government proposals prior to establishing income-generating projects, or to bring pressure to bear through appropriate channels to forestall investments at the national level which could result in lost opportunities for rural employment.

In many countries, there are now specific government departments dealing with the development and promotion of small-scale and village industries and yet, with one or two exceptions (school uniforms in Botswana, day-care equipment in Jamaica, various industries in India) the case studies show little evidence of use being made of existing government schemes.

Before commencing projects it would be useful for directors

to investigate the existence of any planned developments at national level which could affect the success of the project, and also the ways in which projects could make use of existing government policies in support of rural industry.

Macro-economics   Finally, there seems to be little evidence in the case studies to suggest that any great thought is given at the time of project selection to issues such as trends in demand (income elasticities of demand), or global issues, such as rising oil prices, and yet these can (or should) have a significant bearing on choice of activity and the use of technology within activities. For example, demand trends would affect choice in the direction of services rather than manufacture of foods or cloth, while rising oil prices could suggest investment in equipment powered by renewable energy sources rather than diesel/electricity.

A final set of questions that project directors need to ask relates to the impact that a project can be expected to have at the macro level. Would the advantages for participants be more than outweighed by harmful impact on rural women elsewhere in the economy? Is demand for the chosen product growing sufficiently to allow increased productivity, without causing displacement of labour? Are project economics likely to be significantly affected by trends, such as rising oil prices? The writer hopes that concrete data based on experiences with implementing income-generating projects for women can help to pin-point the nature and causes of the difficulties that may be encountered, thus assisting in the process of planning for further projects. It will be clear, however, that while the experiences of others may be useful in helping to overcome some of the more obvious pitfalls in implementation, there are no hard and fast rules which guarantee success. An indication can be given of the questions which should be asked: the answers can only be supplied, if at all, in the particular location in which the project is to be implemented.

While projects such as those described here can provide the basis for sustained employment and income for hundreds of rural women, and should thus be encouraged, they are in themselves unlikely to tackle the problem on an adequate scale.

The need is for the technologies and methodologies which have been utilized in successful projects to be replicated on a widespread basis, and for the creation of the correct economic and policy environment to allow this to occur.

REFERENCES FOR CASE STUDIES

1. FOOD, DRINK AND TOBACCO
- Page 16 Date-Bah, Eugenia; *Rural Women, Their Activities and Technology in Ghana: An Overview* (Geneva, 1LO, WEP 2-22/WP.87).
- 18 *Ibid*.
- 19 King-Akerele, Olubanke; *Traditional Palm Oil Processing, Women's Role and the Applications of Appropriate Technology: Ivory Coast, Sierra Leone, Cameroons*. (FAO/ECA/ATRCW, 1981, Addis Ababa).
- 22 Corbett, S., 'A new peanut oil-press machine fails to improve older methods' *VITA NEWS* April 1981.
- 23 Carr, M., 'Report on a Visit to Jamaica, Barbados and Guyana on behalf of women and Development Unit of the University of the West Indies,' (London ITDG, 1980); and personal communications with Sybil Patterson, University of Guyana, 1983.
- 25 Fennelly Levy, M., *Bringing Women into the Community Development Process: A Pragmatic Approach*. Save the Children, Occasional Papers 2, Westport, 1981.
- 26 Axtell, B., 'Visit to Bangladesh, Nepal and Sri Lanka, 1981' (Rugby, ITDG/ITIS, 1981).
- 28 Jain, D., 'Pappad Rollers of Lijjat' in Jain D., *Women's Quest for Power* (Delhi, Vikas, 1980).
- 30 Gill, G.J. & Sultana, W., *Women's Role in Small Farm Resource Management: A Case Study in Joydebpur, Bangladesh*. (Agricultural Development Council, Dhaka, 1982).
- 31 'A Bakery for Bomani', *REPORTS Magazine*, July 1980.
- 32 Personal Communication with Philip Walker, ex-IVS Manager of Service of Serowe Bakery Project.
- 34 MCC, *Job Creation Programme, Bangladesh*, Report N.2. 1981-1982.
- 37 Fennelly Levy, M., *op.cit*.
- 38 Bergvall, A., 'When the answer is a bottle' *UNICEF NEWS*.
- 39 Devadas, R.P., 'Appropriate Technology with Reference to

Page Infant Weaning Foods', in *Proceedings of First Asian Household Nutrition Appropriate Technology Conference*, Sri Lanka, 1981.
40 Oyawale, F., 'Palmwine—drink of the gods', *Africa Woman* No. 33 May/June 1981.
41 Appropriate Technology Development Institute, *Annual Reports* 1981/82 and 1982/83 (Lae, ATDI, 1982/83); and Carr, M., *Intermediate Technology in Papua New Guinea* (London, ITDG, forthcoming).

2. CLOTH, CLOTHING AND FIBRES
    45 Sinha, F. and Sinha, S., *Woollen Textile Production in the Kumaon Hills*, A Review of the ITIS/ATDA Wool-Spinning Project. (Rugby, ITIS, 1983).
    49 Evans, R., 'Visit to India Nov/Dec 1982' (Rugby, ITIS, 1982).
    50 CUSO, Project Bulletin on Shinyanga Tie and Dye Co-operative in Tanzania.
    51 Caughman, S., *New Skills for Rural Women: an example of transfer of traditional technology*. (AFSC, mimeo, 1978).
    52 Dhamija, J., *Women and Handicrafts: Myth and Reality* (New York, Seeds Report No.4, 1981).
    54 Fennelly Levy, M., *op.cit.*
    55 Holtermann, S., *Intermediate Technology in Ghana* (ITDG, London 1980); and personal communication with John Powell, Director of TCC, 1983.
    56 Winburn, T.T., 'Ericulture: Handicraft for the Poor', *Appropriate Technology* Vol 6 No.1 May 1979.
    58 CUSO, *Project Bulletins* on: Women's Tailoring Cooperative, Manyori Village in Tanzania; Tailor's Project, Bupandaglia in Tanzania; and Msikatetamaa Women's Sewing Cooperative in Itala District, Tanzania.
    59 O'Regan, F., 'Women in Development Project, Swaziland' in O'Regan, F., and Hellinger, D., *Assisting the Smallest Economic Activities of the Poor: Part II Case Studies: Africa*. (Accion International/AITEC, Cambridge, Mass., 1980).
    60 Discussion Paper prepared by Bothakga Knitwear for Commonwealth Secretariat Workshop on 'Employment Strategies for Women', Chandinagar, April, 1983.
    61 Herklotts, J., Report on a Visit to India, Oct. 1981, (ITIS Rugby, 1981).
    63 Risseeuw, C., *The Wrong End of the Rope: Women Coir Workers in Sri Lanka*. (Research Project Women and Development, Leiden 1980).

3. BUILDING MATERIALS, HOUSING AND HOUSEHOLD GOODS

Page 68 Sakula, J.H., *Sisal Cement Roofing in Eastern and Southern Africa*. (Rugby, ITIS, 1982).
70 Kaufman, M., *From Lorena to a Mountain of Fire* (Dian Desa, Yogjakarta, 1983); and Carr, M., Report on Visit to Dian Desa, 1983 (ITDG, London, 1983).
72 Joseph, S., *A Preliminary Assessment of the Impact of Stove Programmes*. (ITDG, London 1983); and *Cookstove News*, Vol 2 No.3 1982; Vol 2 No.2 1983. (The newsletter of Approvecho Institute).
73 CUSO Project Bulletin on Women's Soap-making Co-operative in Tanzania.
74 Caugham, S., 'Soap-making—the experiences of a women's cooperative in Mali' *Appropriate Technology* Vol 7 No.3.
79 Cole, J., 'Providing access to new skills and modern techniques', *Carnets de l'enfance*, Vol No. 38, 1976; and Date-Bah, E., *op-cit*.

4. OTHER CONSUMER GOODS
83 Antrobus, P., *Hanover Street: An Experiment to Train Women in Welding and Carpentry*. (New York, Seeds Report, 1980).
86 Tinker, I. and Raynolds, L.T., *Integrating Family Planning and Women's Enhancement Activities: Theory and Practice*. (Washington, USAID/Equity Policy Centre, 1982).
87 Notes following 1983 Visit of ITDG's AT Institutions Advisor.

5. OTHER PRODUCTIVE ACTIVITIES
91 Lawmark, S., 'Women's contribution to intensive household production', *ADAB NEWS* Vol IX No. 2 March/April 1982.
94 Personal Communication from Martin Whiteside, ex-IVS project worker at Mahalapye Development Trust Gardens Group.
96 Simi, N., *Report on the National Workshop on the FAO/ESCAP Inter-Country Project for the Promotion and Training of rural Women in Income Raising Group Activities* (Apia, 1983).
97 Thrupp, Lori Ann, 'Women, Wood and Work: The Imperative for Equity in Overcoming a Deeper Energy Crisis' (IDS, mimeo, 1983).

Page 99 Carr, M., Report of Mission Undertaken at Request of the Ministry of Housing and Social Services, Nairobi, Kenya, 1976. (ATRCW, Addis Ababa, 1976).
100 Akhtar, Syed Jameba 'Two Group Stories' *ADAB NEWS* Vol VI, No. 12 December 1979.
100 Allan, D.A., 'Goats and Kids', *UNICEF NEWS*.
101 Md. Lugman, 'Starter fund loans to landless families' *ADAB NEWS* March 1980.
103 Carr, M., Report on 1976 Mission to Kenya, *op-cit*.
106 Nelson, N., *Productive and Income Generating Activities for Third World Women*. (UNICEF, September 1979).

6. SERVICES
    108 CARE in Bangladesh, Women's Development Programme. Mimeod Report, Dhaka, 1982.
    109 Hoskins, M. & Weber, F., *Appropriate Technology Efforts in the Field: Issues Reconsidered Part II. Household Level Appropriate Technology for Women*. (Office of Women in Development, AID, 1982).
    110 Government of The Gambia/ODA, The Gambia Food Strategy Report; Review of Food and Nutrition in the First National Development Plan. (London ODA, 1981).
    111 Khan, S., Evaluation Report on Trainers' Training Programme for Women Group Leaders of Grameen Bank Project. (GBP, Dhaka 1982).
    112 MCC, Job Creation Programme, *op-cit*; and notes from author's visit to Bangladesh in 1982.
    113 Kreerim, J., *Village Women Organize: The Mraru Bus Service*. (New York, Seeds Project, 1980).

SOURCES FOR FURTHER INFORMATION

JOURNALS
- *ADAB NEWS* from Agricultural Development Agencies in Bangladesh, 79 Road 11A, Dhanmondi, Dhaka—9, Bangladesh.
- *Africa Woman* from Africa Journal Ltd, Kirkman House, 54A Tottenham Court Road, London W1P 0BT.
- *Appropriate Technology* from Intermediate Technology Development Group, 9 King Street, London WC2E UK.
- *Carnets de l'enfance* from UNICEF, Villa Le Bocage, Palais des Nations, 1211 Genève 10, Switzerland.
- *Ceres* from FAO, Via della Terme di Caracalla 00100, Rome, Italy.
- *Cookstove News* from Aprovecho Institute, 442 Munroe Street, Eugene, Oregon 97402, USA.
- *REPORTS* Magazine from International Research Council, 60 Queen Street, P.O. Box 8500, Ottawa, Canada K1G 3H9.
- *SEEDS* reports from SEEDS, P.O. Box 3923, Grand Central Station, New York, N.Y. 10163, USA.
- *The Exchange Report* from The Exchange, 26 East 22nd Street, New York, NY 10010, USA.
- *UNICEF NEWS* from UNICEF, United Nations, New York, NY 10017, USA.
- *VITA NEWS* from Volunteers in Technical Assistance, 1815 North Lynn Street, Rosslyn, Virginia 22209, USA.

OTHER PUBLICATIONS AND PROJECT INFORMATION
- Accion International AITEC publication from Accion International/AITEC, 10C North Auburn Street, Cambridge, Mass. 02138, USA.
- African Friends Service Committee project information, 1501 Cherry Street, Philadelphia, Pennsylvania 19102, USA.
- American Home Economics Association Publication from 2010 Massachusetts Avenue North West, Washington D.C. 20036, USA.
- ATRCW reports, books and project information from African Training and Research Centre for Women, ECA, Box 3001, Addis Ababa, Ethiopia.
- CARE, Bangladesh information from CARE Mission, P.O. Box 226, Dhaka 2, Bangladesh.

- Commonwealth Secretariat papers from Office of the Adviser on Women in Development, Commonwealth Secretariat, Malborough House, Pall Mall, London SW17 5HY.
- CUSO project information from Canadian University Service Overseas, 151 Slater Street, Ottawa, Ontario K1P 5H5, Canada.
- Dian Desa, P.O. Box 19, Bulaksumur, Yogyakarta, Indonesia.
- Grameen Bank Project, 2G Shyamoli, Dhaka 7, Bangladesh.
- IDS publications from Institute of Development Studies, University of Sussex, Falmer, Brighton, UK.
- ITDG and ITIS reports, books and project information from Intermediate Technology Development Group, 9, King Street, London WC2, UK.
- IVS project information from International Voluntary Service, Ceresole House, 53 Regent Road, Leicester LE1 6YL, UK.
- MCC Publications from Mennonite Central Committee, 1/1 Block 'A', Mohammadpur, Dhaka 2, Bangladesh.
- Research Project Women and Development, Ryksuniversiteit Leiden, Stationsplain 10, 2312 AK Leiden, The Netherlands.
- Save the Children publications and project information from Save the Children Federation, 54 Wilton Road, Westport, Conn. 06880, USA.
- USAID Women in Development publications from Office for Women in Development, USAID, Department of State, Washington DC 20523, USA.